§ The ph
1920 but
at the outbreak ~~~ ~~~ ~~~ ~~~
London, he arrived in Rio de Janeiro with his wife and
parents-in-law at the end of 1940. The Flussers settled
in São Paulo, where they lived for thirty-two years. In
the early 1970s they moved back to Europe, settling
first in Italy and then in Robion, France, where they
lived until Vilém Flusser's untimely death in a car crash
in 1991, after leaving a symposium in Prague.
§ While living in Brazil, Flusser wrote for Brazilian
periodicals and taught at several academic institutions,
including the University of São Paulo, the Brazilian
Institute of Philosophy, and the Institute of Technology
and Aeronautics. His first two books, *Language and
Reality* and *The History of the Devil*, were published
in Brazil during the 1960s. In the late 1970s and
1980s Flusser travelled throughout Europe, lecturing
and participating in conferences and symposia
and publishing his best-known titles. He came to
prominence in the field of media philosophy after
publishing his seminal book *Towards a Philosophy of
Photography* in 1983, which was followed shortly by *Into
the Universe of Technical Images* in 1985 and *Does Writing
Have a Future?* in 1987. § A polyglot, Flusser wrote
in four languages: German, Portuguese, English, and
French. The "Metaflux//Vilém Flusser" collection
aims to present high quality translations of Flusser's
Brazilian writings to an international readership. These
include his academic courses, monographs, essays, and
letters, as well as works originally written in English.
§ The "Metaflux//Vilém Flusser" collection is possible
due to the generous support of Miguel Gustavo Flusser.

VILÉM FLUSSER
GROUNDLESS

Metaflux 2017

METAFLUX // VILÉM FLUSSER

Bodenloss: Uma Autobiografia Filosófica

©1973 Vilém Flusser
©2017 Miguel Flusser

Edited and translated from the Portuguese original by
Rodrigo Maltez Novaes

1. Communication Theory; 2. Philosophy; 3. Autobiography

First edition ©2017 Metaflux Publishing

This book has been published with support from the
Brazilian Ministry of Culture / National Library Foundation

Obra publicada com o apoio do
Ministério da Cultura do Brasil / Fundação Biblioteca Nacional

 MINISTÉRIO DA CULTURA
Fundação BIBLIOTECA NACIONAL

Art and Design by Chagrin
Published by Metaflux Publishing
www.metafluxpublishing.com

Text revision Martha Schwendener and Fiona Hanley

ISBN 978 0 9933272 6 1

Like in so many different ways, I am full of doubts,
and short of formed opinions.

V. Flusser, 1975

A SKETCHED LIFE

§ In the beginning of 1973, Vilém Flusser was commissioned by Ed. Mame, Paris, to write an account of his experiences as a Jewish émigré to Brazil during the Second World War. The original commission was to be published as a book, written from the author's subjective firsthand account of events. However, when Flusser began writing, the project naturally grew and eventually morphed into an autobiography. This book commission coincided with Flusser's permanent move back to Europe, and with his decision to "disengage" with Brazil on a formal level after thirty-two years of engagement with what he called "the Brazilian reality." For this reason, Flusser decided that he would use this opportunity to write a book that could stand as the pivoting point between his former years in Brazil and his future in Europe.

§ On 21 June 1973 he wrote to Milton Vargas describing his initial efforts and intentions with the project:

As for the "autobiography," I share your concerns. I also have prudence and detest striptease. But I thought I should accept Ed. Mame's challenge because once you told me that I should bear witness to those events. (Do you remember it?) If I fictionalise my experiences (as Proust did, for example) I falsify them. You will see in the continuation of the project that I hope to be able to contribute a little for the demystification and de-ideologisation of the Brazilian situation both here and in Brazil, if the book ever comes to be published in S. Paulo. ... Afterall, my biography drove, for decades, towards yours, to then run parallel. Read what I am writing as if you were discovering one of your roots. Just as I am discovering my roots in your biography. In other words, I believe that friendship means: to create a joint biography. ... And one more thing: to write a biography at 53 means "to make biography," in the same sense as when Hegel says that to write the history of philosophy means "to make history and philosophy."

§ Flusser's gesture in writing the book was, therefore, to be one of analysis and projection. As analysis, the intention was to write a book that would allow Flusser to mentally revisit his past and analyse from a distanced position the development of his own work in relation to the events of his life and his interaction with others. The intention was also to bear witness not only to the events of the Second World War, and their aftermath, but also to the military coup d'etat that took place in brazil in 1964, which ultimately played a role in Flusser's decision to return to Europe. As projection, the intention was to look forward and present to the world his future intellectual plans, which were associated to the intellectuals and artists he had recently met and befriended in Europe.

§ On 16 August 1973 Flusser wrote a letter to Dora Ferreira da Silva where he describes for the first time his intended structure for the book:

Rodrigo Maltez Novaes

Here is the structure of the thing: I: The loss of grounding (Prague, Nazism, the War, São Paulo 1940-45) II: Search for grounding (philosophy, Wittgenstein and Kafka, yoga, Brazilian nature 1945-50) III: Brazilian dialogic engagement (1950-70) IV: Brazilian discursive engagement (1950-70): lectures, conferences, published and unpublished essays, actions such as the Art Biennial, the Folha de São Paulo *and the* O Estado de São Paulo *newspapers, FAAP V: Painful disengagement and the search for "Self" (1970s -): Christianity, Judaism, Neo-Nazism, a return to Phenomenology, A. Moles, A. Bonnier, J. Berger etc. Fundamental subject: faith in despair. Epiphenomenal subjects: mass culture, kitsch, Brazil, scientism, futurology, "The New Left," crisis in art. Rhythm: elegiac. Style: existential phenomenology. Method: the analysis of conscious memory. Mood: unhappy love. Aim: to turn my own life into a laboratory for others.*

§ This was to be, in many ways, an experimental project. Flusser wrote several letters to Milton Vargas, Dora Ferreira da Silva and José Bueno on the subject, seeking advice from them on several points. As he completed the chapters, the drafts were sent to Brazil for his friends' appreciation and comments. However, this exchange soon took on a negative turn. The main section of the book is a series of portraits of some of his closest friends, and Flusser decided to send the draft of each portrait to the person he had written about hoping to receive their reaction. Vargas and da Silva both reacted very strongly against what they read, therefore, the process turned into one of tension between Flusser and his friends. Even so, Flusser continued to write and insist with Vargas that he should edit the text and seek a publisher in Brazil for the book. Vargas was perhaps Flusser's closest and most loyal friend. Despite having a negative opinion of the project, Vargas was never offended and never abandoned Flusser. Da Silva, on the other hand, was deeply offended and cut off communication with Flusser for a while.

§ Later, on 27 November 1973, Flusser wrote to Bueno, still seeking a positive sounding board for his project, someone who could give him the feedback he needed. In this letter Flusser reworks some of the structure of the project and goes further to explain how the other friends had received the drafts:

[I] have started to write the autobiography, under the title Certificate of Groundlessness. *This is the structure: I. Passivity and suffering: (a) Prague, (b) London, (c) S. Paulo up to 1950. II. Activity and engagement: (a) Productive dialogues with Bloch, Vargas, Flexor, you, Dora, Mira, G. Rosa, Campos brothers, Reale, Ely, and the youth. (b) discourses as lectures, essays, books (c) praxis as engagement with academia, biennials, tv etc. III. Disenchantment and disengagement: (a) ending the situation, Estado, Folha, biennial etc. (b) European experiences, A. Moles, A. Bonnier, A. Berger, Minkhoff, F. Forrest etc. (c) ironic discourses, (my current books). So far I have written with head, heart, and entrails to reach II. (a) Campos brothers. (I have already written your section and Milton has the corresponding text.) I have always*

been aware of the problem, from which the most terrify *is that my gaze freezes (thing-fies in this sense) my [dialo* *partners and myself. But I hoped that this freezing would be* *compensated by the heat of emotion that surfaces. I gradually* *sent the manuscript to the editor [in Paris] and to Milton. The* *editor is excited, thinks that this is an exceptional text, and* *encourages me to continue at full speed. All of my European* *friends think the same. (Moles says that it is a "masterpiece.")* *Vargas thinks that the first half is a type of "I was Hitler's* *whore" [account], that the second [half] is pure hatred, and* *that the portraits of my interlocutors are subjective caricatures.* *Dora has broken off her friendship because of Vicente's portrait.* *(Milton has also stopped answering.) I have stopped writing* *purely out of confusion. I feel the need to write this account,* *but I can't hurt the ones that are dear to me. José, please, try* *to read what I've written, ask Milton and tell me what you* *honestly think. ...This autobiography is something else: it is a* *type of repayment for everything I have received during my* *life. But the ones I'm paying back think I'm betraying them.* *Now I understand [the expression] "quand-même" from* *a different angle. When I started I thought of myself as a* *miniature St Augustin. Now I see myself as a miniature* *Dante (of the* Inferno*). Please help me.*

§ Flusser's internal and external conflicts in relation to the project continued until the beginning of 1974, when he eventually abandoned the text and decided not to publish what he had written up to that point. Bueno eventually answered Flusser's pleas for help and served as a neutral bridge between Vargas and Flusser, helping them to soothe the conflict. With Vargas, despite the disagreements

the nature of the project, Flusser asked for
' primarily about the style of the work.
he very start, his intention was to apply an
ːntal writing style in order to dissolve, in
 the focus on the author's perspective.
..tions in the letter to Bueno, Flusser was
..ore than aware of the subjective nature of his
account, however, he sought to at least attempt
a formal dissolution of such subjectivity, if only
from an aesthetic angle. For this effect Flusser
chose to use only an indefinite personal pronoun
throughout the first and second sections of the
book, which in Portuguese is *a gente*, in German *man*,
and in French *on*. Therefore, for this translation,
the English pronoun "one" became the obvious
choice. However, for the last three chapters, under
the section heading Discourse, Flusser returned to
the first person definite pronoun "I" throughout,
therefore, the reader will notice a significant change
in style in those chapters.

§ This translation was done from the Brazilian
edition published by Anna Blume in 2007, which
was the first edition of the Portuguese version.
There are two corresponding original versions, one
in German and another in Portuguese. For the first
German edition, published by Bollmann in 1992,
two years after Flusser's death, the editors chose to
change the structure of Flusser's text by sectioning
it into four distinct parts: Monologue, Dialogue,
Discourse, and Reflections. The Brazilian edition
also followed the same structure and included the

last essays as translations of their German versions. However, as Flusser's letters clearly indicate, this was not the structure intended. The section titled Reflections became a compilation of four extra essays that also have an autobiographical focus, but which were written towards the end of the author's life. Had Flusser decided to take up the project again towards the end of his life he would probably have changed the entire thing, or possibly rewritten it. But to speculate as to what Flusser would have done had he decided to publish the book before he died is pointless. However, for this edition, the decision was made to restore the structure according to the original structure of the typescripts, without any additions. The unfinished project, as it stands, is already a very powerful portrait of the author's life, work, and thought process. Therefore, no changes or additions are necessary.

§ The original title, which Flusser also mentions in the letters, was *Certificate of Groundlessness*. This was meant as a reference to two concepts from German Existentialism: *Bodenlos* and *Bodenlosigkeit*. Both terms are normally translated to English as *Groundless* and *Groundlessness* respectively, especially in the translations of philosophical texts. The German and Brazilian editions were eventually published under the same title *Bodenlos*, which we decided to keep but using the English equivalent *Groundless*. The German edition also added a dedication in the beginning of the book, which reads *Uxori omnia mea* (to my wife, who is everything to me), however, this dedication originally appeared in the first edition of *The History of the Devil* (Martins, S. Paulo, 1965). It was Flusser's custom to add dedications in his books, but whenever he did this, the dedications always appear typed on the same page as the table of contents. With *Groundless* this is not the case. The dedication appears only in handwriting on the German typescript, but the handwriting is not by Flusser or his widow Edith. This suggests that the dedication was added probably by the editor of the German edition, or by somebody else. Since the Brazilian edition does not have this dedication, and since it is not clear whether Flusser intended to have it in this book, we have, therefore, decided not to included it.

§ This edition follows Flusser's original typescript very closely and, for this reason, discards the changes made by the Brazilian editor. Like the moving of paragraphs between some chapters, and the misspelling of some German terms. Therefore, this is the first edition of Flusser's autobiography project to reach an international audience as close as possible to Flusser's original intentions.

Rodrigo Maltez Novaes
2017

CERTIFICATE OF GROUNDLESSNESS

§ "The absurd" is a term that originally means "groundless," in the same sense as "rootless," just like a plant in a vase is groundless. Flowers in a vase, on the dinner table, are examples of absurd life. If we wish to intuit these flowers, we can feel their tendency to sprout roots, and to push them into any soil. The rootless flowers' tendency is the climate of groundlessness. This book shall attest to this climate.

§ "The absurd" is a term that means, in the majority of cases, "groundless," in the same sense as "meaningless," just like the planetary system is groundless when we ask, "Why do the planets orbit around the Sun in that abyssal void?" Mercury and Venus are examples of absurd functionalism. One feels strongly tempted to compare this system with the administrative apparatus in function of which we live most of our lives. Meaningless motion, with the void as a horizon, is the climate of groundlessness. This book shall attest to this climate.

§ "The absurd" is a term that also means "groundless" in the same sense as "without reason," just like the sentence "two times two is four at seven o'clock in São Paulo" is groundless. This sentence is an example of absurd thinking, and it leads us to the sensation of hovering above the abyss, in which the concepts of "true" and "false" do not apply. This sentence is groundless because it would be absurd to say that it is either true or false, since it is simultaneously both and neither. This hovering sensation is the climate of groundlessness. This book shall attest to this climate.

§ These examples from botany, astronomy, and logic are meant to introduce the reader to the climate of this book; a climate that we all know from personal experience, although we may attempt to suppress it. This is the climate of religiosity. And all religions emerged from this climate, since they are methods to generate grounding. But this is also a dangerous climate for all religions, because the acid of absurdity corrodes the grounding provided by religion in such climate. In the final analysis, all of our problems are religious. If we find ourselves groundless, we seek a religious solution, but never find it. And if we feel any grounding beneath our feet (thanks to a religion, or any other religion substitute, or simply, thanks to the obscuring force of daily life), we lose the true climate of religiosity (however, perhaps this formulation is itself the result of being groundless).

§ Indirectly, we all know this climate from personal experience. For example, through Surrealism, Existentialism, and The Theatre of the Absurd. There were times when this climate predominated within cultural manifestations, for example, towards the end of Antiquity, or the Middle Ages, and today. These were times of rupture. However: these cultural manifestations of groundlessness both reveal and conceal the truth. Whenever groundlessness becomes a theme for public discussion, it ceases to be what it is. Groundlessness is the experience of loneliness, and it melts away when publicly discussed.

§ The experience of groundlessness cannot be conveyed in literature, philosophy, and art without being falsified. Groundlessness can only be circumscribed in these forms, so that it may be partially grasped. But it is possible to attest it both directly and autobiographically, in the hope that such document may serve as a mirror to others. That is the motive for this book (and not, one hopes, vanity or the need for self-affirmation).

§ We all know the climate of groundlessness from personal experience, and if we deny it, then we have managed to repress it (a dubious victory). But there are those who find themselves, so-to-speak, objectively groundless, either because they were taken from their reality by external forces, or because they spontaneously abandoned an apparently real situation, which they diagnosed to be phantasmagoria. Therefore, there are those who have either fallen into, or deliberately chosen, groundlessness. These are the ones that can serve as laboratories for others. They exist more intensely, if "to exist" is interpreted as "to live on the outside." This book shall attest to one such intense type of existence.

PRAGUE BETWEEN THE WARS

§ The imperial city of Prague on the Vltava River,
with its Gothic castle and its Baroque suburb
on one side of the city, and its Gothic rooftops
and industrial suburbs on the other side, has a
marked personality unlike any other city. And
as such, it induces one to rethink the difference
between "civilisation" and "culture." Culture is
the product of agriculture; a "harvest" (*colere*)
of things gathered from nature. Civilisation is a
product of urban life; the attempt to meaningfully
inform the life of the "citizen" (*civis*); to form,
and not, to harvest. Only a few cities have this
formative power. The majority are centres for their
rural surroundings: a cultural focal point. Only
a few cities made the leap to become cradles of
civilisation, and Prague is one of them. This leap
could be sociologically explained, however, such
an explanation is unnecessary. Prague's civilising
character immediately shines through in the form
of beauty: a beauty independent from the size and
landscape of the city. Paris has this beauty in its
majestic largesse, Florence in its moderation, and
Classical Athens had it, although it was a village.
Whoever visits these cities must either love or hate
them. And whoever was born and/or lived in one
of these cities must accept them as the centre of the
world. *Sum civis Pragensis.*

§ Prague imposes an indelible mark upon its
citizens. One may attempt to deny Prague (like
Rilke), to accept it as destiny (like Kafka), or to
ansform it into a task (like Neruda), but for those
who live outside the city's walls, the citizens of
Prague will be forever Pragueans. The characteristic
trait of Prague is that its essence overcomes all
national, social, and religious differences: it does
not matter if one is Czech, German, Jew, Christian,
Protestant, Marxist, bourgeois, or proletarian.
Before all else, one is Praguean. Prague is an
existential climate, and every division, with its
multiple tensions, happens in such a climate.

§ However, the tensions are many and violent. Only
they can explain the incredible richness of Praguean
civilisation. Between the two Great Wars Prague
was the centre of a new Czech culture (inspired by
Masaryk), of European Jewish cultural life, and of a
trend in German culture that allowed the monarchic
tradition of the Habsburgs to flourish. These three
cultures were mutually fertilised through struggles
and collaborations, which provoked a tremendous
richness of ideas. One only need think of the
Prague Circle, Kafka, Rilke, Čapek's experimental
theatre, phenomenology, Einstein at the University,
and psychoanalysis with all of its varying schools.
To grow up in that ambiance, to feel the tension
within oneself, and to actively participate in all
of it from puberty, seemed obvious to a son of
intellectual Jews, but it only revealed itself as a
privileged situation much later.

Vilém Flusser

§ The linguistic aspect can shed some light on the privilege: it was taken for granted that one had two first languages. One spontaneously shifted from Czech to German, and thus one was a natural participant of both Western and Eastern Europe. One's evolving spirit did not experience the fundamental differences between the Slavic and Germanic languages as differences, but as complements (for example: the specific function of the Czech verb and the agglutinating capacity of the German noun, reminiscent of Greek). One thought spontaneously within categories of two worlds that seemed irreconcilable to others. Spontaneously: because one thought in the Praguean way (by the way: Kafka and Rilke are incomprehensible to those who cannot hear their Czech connotations, and the same is valid, *mutatis mutandis*, for Čapek and Bezruče).

§ The privilege becomes apparent, negatively, in the question of self-identification: was one Czech, German, or Jew? Obviously: we were all Pragueans and that was our ground. But upon this ground, the three alternatives posed themselves as choices. Or were they somehow imposed? And did one have the right to place Judaism upon the same line as the other alternatives? Clearly: one was not German in the same way a Saxon peasant was, or Czech in the same way a Moravian peasant was. Equally: one was not Jewish in the same way an inhabitant of a small Polish town or of Frankfurt was. One was an assimilated Jew. But assimilated to what, since

Prague was not something to which one had to assimilate? Prague was within us.

§ Any type of national self-identification was seen as archaism. One was a born internationalist because one could intimately experience the ridiculousness of any national differentiation. And this was not a socialist type of internationalism, which sought to overcome nationality through revolution. Nationality was already overcome by the fact that one was Praguean. But such an attitude could not be sustained. Nazism in Germany usurped the right to speak on behalf of the Germans and many Pragueans yielded to this demagogy. As a reaction, a no less noble type of Czech nationalism emerged in Prague. So should one deny one's own German aspect? and would this mean to accept that Nazism represented Germany? or should one opt for Czech nationalism? and would this mean to accept Nazism as something necessarily negative? However, it was impossible to ignore the fact that a vulgar type of German nationalism was readying itself to kill us. The alternative was Zionism. But Zionism was dubious, because the Praguean *forma mentis* had already overcome this type of nationalism, since it was a reaction to anti-Semitism. And because Zionism conceded to Judaism a role contrary to the Praguean one: to be a bridge between peoples. Zionism meant bourgeois alienation. But above all, it meant one would have to abandon Prague, which was inconceivable. Prague grounded one's reality and the thought of living in agrarian collectives in Palestine was nothing but fantasy. However, despite this, Zionism imposed itself as a method to oppose the caricature of the Jew projected by Nazism (a ridiculous but dangerous caricature) with an image of a dignified Jewish life. Therefore, this was not Zionism as escapism, but as a struggle for dignity.

§ However, one's engagement with Zionism had reservations. (From today's perspective, it is curious to admit that the Arab problem did not represent any reservations. The Arabs, as well as actual Palestine, were beyond the horizon of Praguean life.) One's reservations were superficially Marxist but fundamentally religious. One was spontaneously Marxist and studied Marxist literature. There were several reasons for this: one was young and believed that Marxism could change the world scientifically towards a new Man. One was Praguean and believed that Marxism could result in a cultural synthesis, of which Prague was already an example in miniature. One was Jewish and believed that Marxism elevated Jewish Messianism to a scientifically founded universal level. One was religiously famished and believed that Marxism represented a system in which all religious problems (and especially the problem of existential engagement) were resolved. Therefore: one was Marxist due to Marxistically false reasons; due to bourgeois alienation and not as a revolt against capitalist oppression. At the time, this type of Marxism was referred to as "Parlour Marxism" and the real Marxists derided it.

§ Effectively, this false Marxism did not prevent the following: it did not prevent one's repulsion of the Soviet system, especially against the Moscow Trials. It did not prevent one's critical attitude in relation to the Soviet role in the Spanish Civil War. It did not prevent one's distrust of Marxist theses within science, especially in biology and psychology. It did not prevent one's feeling that as philosophy, Marxism is not sufficiently profound. But, above all, it did not prevent one's engagement with Zionism.

§ Curiously, the awareness of being a false Marxist was always present. True Marxism did not fit in Prague, not even to one's own situation in the city. Marxism did not fit in Prague because the government was left-leaning, social injustices were tolerable, and the standard of living, after the overcoming of the economic crisis, was acceptable. Marxism did not fit to one's own situation because as the son of intellectuals, one was neither capitalist nor connected to the masses. One belonged to the elite, but not in the economic sense. A Marxist revolution would not bring any personal good or ill. One was Marxist not for political reasons, but for religious ones.

§ Judaism as a religion provided practically nothing. The few remaining rituals, in decadent tradition, represented an empty type of formalism. They exerted an aesthetic attraction, but one knew that the aesthetic aspect concealed their religious meaning. Jewish texts were inaccessible due to one's mere fragmentary knowledge of Hebrew, and for being rendered in an impenetrable style. The Orthodox Jews of Prague were of Galician origin, and subsequently stranger than one's Catholic and Protestant fellow citizens. Essentially, one was not Jewish in a religious sense. However, from a negative perspective, Judaism as a religion was important because it blocked one's access to Christianity by shedding light upon the dogmatic side of Christianity and obfuscating its evangelist side, by shedding light upon the para-Pagan side of Christianity and obfuscating its mystical side, by concealing the close parentage between Judaism and Christianity, and by not allowing a full view of the figure of Christ – but above all, by not allowing one to forget the many persecutions of the Jews in the name of Christianity. Rationally speaking, one knew that these persecutions could never have been Christian, because Christianity could never be anti Semitic. However, emotionally, one could not synthesise the idea of Christian love with the experience of priests that incited the *pogroms*.

§ One could be neither Jewish nor Christian, so Marxism was the only remaining option. That was a typical situation for Jews between the two World Wars, but in Prague this acquired a certain level of specificity. In Prague, Marxism meant engagement in favour of a supra-nationalism. One was Praguean Marxist and the problem of being either Czech or German disappeared. One was Praguean Marxist, the appropriate religion for Praguean Jews, but which was a far too fragile material to serve as shelter against the barbarians in Germany. Therefore, one chose Marxist Zionism and continued to be supra-national, which meant to affirm Judaism in spite of Nazism. This was a solution doomed to failure, because Zionism negated both Marxism and Prague, the existential ground of one's life.

§ To be Praguean is a religious type of Being (whoever has read Kafka knows it). Prague is a profoundly religious city, the opposite of Paris, which hardly deserves a prayer. Not only its churches, synagogues, cemeteries, and bridges, but also every corner of the old city of Prague breathes with religious trembling. Prague is a mystical city where the dialectic "God/Devil" is made manifest not only architecturally, but also through several myths and in the minds of its inhabitants: the dialectic between ardent faith and sharp intellect. Every problem is manifested within this dialectic (just think of Rilke's *Elegies*). This chiaroscuro – simultaneously Gothic, Baroque, and Surrealist – was the Pragueans' ground: a dialectic, and its ironic overcoming, as the ground for a profoundly rooted existence (just think of Čapek's theatre). Hence, this religious atmosphere insistently invited an engagement with philosophy.

§ To philosophise as a young man in Prague before the Second World War meant to attempt to dialectically absorb all available trends, especially

the apparently non-dialectical trends such as
"Phenomenology and Existentialism" on one side
and "Linguistics and Neopositivism" on the other,
within an already described Marxist backdrop. This
was a task for a lifetime and it was inebriating. One
believed oneself to be open to the world (reading,
for example, J. Ortega y Gasset), but in hindsight
the Praguean limitation becomes obvious. The
entire French and Anglo-Saxon worlds passed by
merely as shadows on the horizon, and the real
information was limited to German and Russian
cultures. Prague's narrowness was concealed
by its profoundness.

§ Therefore, this is the symptom of being sheltered:
to think one is the epicentre of the world. Clearly:
one knew that this epicentre was in danger. In
the short-term the threat came from the Nazi
barbarians and in the long-term from the profound
changes happening on a global scale. One knew
that, if seen from such a broad perspective, Prague
was an anachronism. However, existentially, one
was not aware of this. Prague was one's reality, and
how could this reality disappear? The approaching
Nazis and the Chinese gathering beyond the
horizon were nothing but fantasy. And this fantasy
would dissolve before the eternal reality of Prague's
city walls. Prague was eternal: if it disappeared,
everything would disappear.

THE NAZI INVASION

§ So everything disappeared. Not in "one fell swoop" (as the Nazis liked to say), but in small bits, and not when the tanks and the slogans "In Prague we drive on the right" in blackletter appeared on the streets. Reality disappeared bit-by-bit, and bit-by-bit it was swallowed by the abyss. Then the headline, "*Finis Austriae*" appeared on the *Prager Tagblatt.* How could one digest that? How could one digest that one's relatives in Vienna, our twin city, were being systematically murdered? The refugees reported the events, which were still unbelievable. This did not fit our experience of Vienna. These things happened in the Middle Ages and in remote Africa (in distant places), but not on *Kärtnerstrasse.* Reality was being invaded by nightmares. One could no longer distinguish between dream and reality. The structure of reality trembled. Nightmares in one's sleep were less terrifying than the daily news. The acceptance of reality became a problem. Everything such as family, friends, university, philosophy, art, and future plans had to be accepted as an illusion, and reality was the fact of imminent death: an ontological task that threatened to overwhelm even the full strength of a young man.

§ One was tempted to close one's eyes to Vienna and hope that all of this would pass. Many fell victim to this temptation. They clung to Prague as to an iceberg floating on warm currents. However, Zionism emerged as a bridge over the abyss. One started to consider an agrarian life in Palestine as a concrete possibility. But one could see that mentally, physically, and by education, one did not have even the slightest aptitude for that. All of a sudden, one became an entirely futile type of existence. From a promising member of the elite, one became a worthless marginal element. The hope of being murdered by the Nazis emerged as the easiest solution. Even so, one's survival instinct fought against this urge to surrender. One studied Hebrew, the geography of Palestine, and agriculture. But one knew that by doing so, one was betraying the very essence of one's *being-in-the-world*.

§ Munich, and the occupation of the so-called "*Sudeten,*" came after. The Czechoslovak Republic's agony was experienced as an epiphenomenon, because what could the death of the Republic represent, against one's own imminent death, against the conviction that one's own survival, if achieved, depended on the abandonment of one's Self? The inability to share in the Czech catastrophe opened an abyss between our Czech friends and us, which added to the abyss that separated us from our German friends. The German friends honestly affirmed their rejection of Nazi barbarism, but they could not honestly deny that the German occupation would bring them advantages, and that a German victory would fulfil unconfessed private tendencies. The Czech friends were losing their freedom and any meaningful future, so they were desperate. But Prague, one's founding ground, continued intact, and its task was to ready itself for the long and arduous struggle against the Nazis. One was losing the ground under one's feet, as one readied oneself to be murdered. Hence, the attitude of one's German friends seemed like betrayal, and one's Czech friends seemed shallow. Prague was split into three groups, and one was relegated to the Jewish component. Prague became unrecognisable. One's friends and relatives who moved to Prague from the occupied *"Sudeten"* also became unrecognisable. These persecuted and terrorised people, with their ill adjusted smiling masks (hiding the fact that they depended on the help of others), could not be the same people one loved and with whom one discussed the future of humanity. It was impossible to talk to them because it felt shameful to unmask them. Simultaneously, one knew that these masks were one's best future in store. The hope of being quickly murdered by the Nazis grew: it became one's only hope.

§ Consequently, one lived feverishly – partly to conceal the crumbling of reality; partly to eliminate the growing religious problems; partly to enjoy life during its last moments. One philosophised like a madman, read incessantly, worked intensely at the university, and engaged with Zionism. One no longer slept because to sleep represented the danger of meeting oneself. That would have been totally despairing and had to be avoided. One spun many fantasies to avoid a wide-eyed vision of reality that was more fantastic than any fantasy.

§ Then the Germans came, which was unbelievable, but anticipated. Their presence was unbelievable, but the changes they caused were even more unbelievable. One had imagined that their presence would represent, in itself, the end of reality. Now one could comprehend that this belief was the result of a lack of imaginative capacity. Their brutal and vulgar presence in their exotic uniforms, with falsely medieval helmets, polished boots, and a fiendish greed for merchandise on shop windows, functioned merely as the catalyst of a radical modification of Prague. Suddenly one found oneself surrounded by quietly and dangerously grinning faces. One became a cornered animal, surrounded by beasts (ex-friends) lying in wait for the first opportunity to attack. Was this a nightmare or was it real? What did all of those people want from us? They sought the opportunity to steal our belongings and to take our positions after the Nazis had murdered us. They were the jackals of the Nazi wolves, who feared the wolves even more than we did, because they had hopes. So was this the "real" Prague, the one that had sheltered us for two thousand years? Was this the ground in which one was rooted?

§ In hindsight, one knows that at that moment one had been staring at the face of Evil, which hides just beneath the surface everywhere at all times, and that at that moment it had just been provoked by the Nazi presence. However, at the time, this distanced understanding was impossible. Despite one's attempt to mobilise all of one's moral and philosophical strength to overcome the wave of meanness, bad faith, open jealousy, and barely hidden pleasure in the misfortune of others, desperation flooded one's heart and soul. One had been reduced to the biological level (according to Nazi "philosophy"), and this was an unforgettable experience.

§ One was a cornered animal, but a "metaphysical" animal nonetheless. One sought to find a deeper meaning to all this. Not by asking, "What will become of us?" but: "What is one's role in such a grotesque situation?" "To save one's life" was not an answer, because that meant to be on the same level as the Nazis. One had to find a more dignified answer. One mobilised within oneself all knowledge and "culture," but the answer did not come. One mobilised every ideal and hope, but the answer did not come. One mobilised the remnants of dormant transcendent faith, but the answer did not come. If this was about saving one's own dignity, then these were nothing but empty forms. Any type of engagement in favour of freedom, humanity, Zionism, or any other culture, was revealed as vanity. Then the decision to escape to the West came, but knowing perfectly well, with unbearable clarity, that such a decision meant the sacrifice of one's dignity in favour of the body's survival.

§ Since escape was so dangerous, one sought excuses to justify it. But what is the meaning of "danger" against practically certain death? Every attempt to transform such a cowardly decision into a heroic act necessarily failed. And the reasonable consideration that being murdered by the Nazis would not bring any benefits to anyone or any ideal also failed. Reasonable considerations are worthless in absurd situations. Subsequently, one would never lose the irrational, but existentially valid conviction that "by right" one should have died in the ovens; that from then on, one lived a borrowed life; that one uprooted oneself from one's own ground (from the ovens) by escaping, and that, "reasonably" (?) the bottomless abyss was one's only possible future. From then on, life became diabolically sacred. From then on, one lived from one's own strengths, and not from the strength that came from one's founding essence. According to myths, this meant to look at oneself diabolically. One became absurdly Titanic – but by escaping, not by choice. Groundlessness had begun.

§ The decision to escape had immediate horrible consequences. One was already dead to one's parents, siblings, friends, and in turn, they were already dead to us. One was a spectre surrounded by spectres. One looked at familiar faces and saw death masks. When, much later, the news of their varying horrible deaths came, such news no longer touched us. The decision to escape had already condemned them to the realm of shadows and their mere murder by the Nazis was nothing but the mechanical execution of a project put in motion by one's escape. The Nazis did not kill one's family; one's own decision to escape did it. One killed them in order to save one's own shadow, this disgusting body. One could never again read Nietzsche's statement of the death of God without self-recognition. Nietzsche became the revelation of what was concealed. However, the two books one took on the escape (the only material belongings) were not by Nietzsche. They were Goethe's *Faust* (because of Mephisto, not Faust), and a Jewish prayer book. One took the prayer book because, apparently, one's already dead mother had put it in one's hands (a mother whose religiosity one had completely ignored) – but also in reality, for reasons one was not aware of then or now. The prayer book (but not *Faust*) was lost during the escape.

§ Thus, Prague died. During the last days one walked through its streets, impregnated by a thousand memories, as if one walked through a strange city. Not much blood had been spilt yet, but the city was already the *Orcus*: a hellish carnival of death and a realm of shadows. Suddenly one had an unexpected sensation: the sensation of vertiginous freedom. From then on one no longer belonged to anyone or anyplace; one was independent. Everything – the city and its inhabitants, the barbarians that occupied it, and one's own family – were nothing but a puppet theatre. One looked at all of this from above. And this view opened up

Groundless

to the horizon of an infinite sky. From then on, everything was possible. And with a bleeding heart, but an open spirit, one fell into such limitless possibility.

Vilém Flusser

ENGLAND UNDER SIEGE

§ Everything turned into shadows. One was a
hologram among holograms of people, cities, and
countries. World history developed as if on a TV
screen and caused the same type of sensational
interest. Was that London? Why not? London or
Johannesburg; it made no difference. They were
empty names. To live in London as a hologram
among holograms was perfectly viable. There were
only two conditions, which could easily be fulfilled.
The first: To earn enough money to nourish the
body. This was easy, because from then on, any type
of work would do. The second: To maintain the
role of distanced observer. This was easy, because
that was one's own situation. Therefore, one lived
well in London during the first months of the war.

§ Despite everything, what was happening was very
interesting. Sensationalist theatre. So Franco won in
Spain? One could not understand why, a thousand
years ago, one felt so emotional in relation to the
Spanish war, as if it were one's own struggle for
survival and dignity. Franco's victory meant nothing
now, not even from the historical point of view, and
even less from the supra-historical point of view
one had taken. A pact between Hitler and Stalin?
So that was the real Marxism: to sacrifice millions
for tactical reasons (aiming at the victory of the
Revolution) and call it "humanism." That served to

liberate us from Marxism. From then on, one had to live without faith, in complete un-religiosity. The war started? The English could not comprehend it, but for us, it was the most natural thing in the world. Nothing was sufficiently fantastic in order to disturb us. Obviously, the war was more dangerous for us than for the English, because in the case of an invasion, one would be murdered. And the war was pernicious to one's family in Prague. But none of it mattered. One was already dead. That is why one had an entirely clear view of the war.

§ Nazism, a *petit-bourgeois* movement financed by international capital (one continued to think in Marxist categories, despite having abandoned it), had built a fantastic ideological edifice that covered up reality. The Germans, but also the capitalist world, had fallen into the trap. The fact was that the war no longer mattered because Europe was no longer the centre of the world. The winner did not matter and the victims were worthless. But Germany would not have won, even if America and the USSR had remained neutral, because even the Germans would not have tolerated the Nazi madness for too long. The only interesting thing was to see how many Nazi victories would be possible thanks to such madness. One was betting that Germany would invade France and England; therefore, that one would be murdered. To bet absurdly on one's own life meant one had become a master of groundlessness.

§ This point of view made it impossible to dialogue
with others. One could not dialogue with the
English because one's views represented defeatism
and a cynical ingratitude towards the refuge granted.
England was going to fight for freedom: did one not
care for it? And one could not talk to the Praguean
refugees because by saying that England would fall,
one was labelled a Nazi. If one said the war made
no difference, one was labelled as inhumane towards
those who remained in Prague. If one said Nazism
was alienation, one was labelled Marxist. There
was no point insisting that one was the opposite
of inhumane, Nazi, or Marxist. Thus came the
discovery of one's loneliness in groundlessness.

§ The fact that the English were grounded did not
represent a problem. They had their Englishness.
But the fact that the refugees had not lost their
ground was a surprise. Did they expect to return to
Prague? Which Prague? The one that was a carnival
of death? Others were Zionists. They expected to
go to Palestine. To do what? To create groundless
reality? Was the fall of our grounding perhaps no
more than a subjective experience?

§ One had to distinguish between the individual
and social dimensions. Apparently, to have lost one's
homeland, family, and position were not enough
to destroy one's grounding. To have lost access to
study philosophy, the possibility of becoming a
writer, and faith in Marxism were also necessary.
The ground gave in only when both components

came together. And when it happened, it was
necessary to hide one's new enthusiasm, which
emerged as a result; the enthusiasm of distanced
observation, which was not the devaluation of
values – and even less the transvaluation of values,
but indifference towards values. That was enthusing.
The Nazis were as interesting as ants; nuclear
physics was as interesting as the English Middle
Ages; and one's own future was as interesting as the
future of parapsychology. This reminded one of
Schopenhauer. But it also reminded one of scientific
rigour and Hell. One's horizons were being opened.
For example, English and North American cultures
opened up, which one had previously ignored.
However, one's conviction that provincialism is not
the result of geographic condition but of framing
emerged even more radically. Regardless of being
from Prague or London, one is provincial if one has
grounding. But whoever has been removed from the
order of things can see the whole world.

§ One could see this was not order but chaos, upon
which several types of order were ridiculously
imposed. It was such a pleasure to observe how
these types of order, like amoebae in a liquid
solution, devoured each other, divided, and thought
of themselves as the centre of everything. One read
Hartmann's ontology with a smile. So physics is
a more fundamental type of order than biology.
Says who? The Hartmann amoeba does. It was
not necessary to wait for the Teilhard de Chardin
amoeba to know that this hierarchy can be inverted.

Every amoeba is transparent, allowing one to see not only the general chaos but also the other amoebae. That was real theatre. And war or biology, religion or psychology, economy or art, among others, were stages for the plays. Kant also emerged, gigantic, but only his *Critique of Pure Reason.* The categorical imperative made no sense.

§ Later on, there were moments when the question of whether this was honest emerged. So be it, one lived ludically. One rejected any type of engagement. One watched the English soldiers returning from Dunkirk as if one were observing plants. One accepted the fall of Paris as one accepted the fall of the Bohrian model (both Paris and the model were shadows). That was excellent. But did one not fear for one's own life? Were Dunkirk and Paris not threats to one's own life? The answer was not an easy one. One could reason that life did not matter, or that Paris was only as important as the model. Pushed into a corner, one wished to die. The fall of Paris represented the hope of death. Biologically, one wished to survive. Thus, the fall of Paris was horrific. Now the Germans could arrive at any moment.

§ Their airplanes were already arriving. Could they be so stupid as to spend all their power on France instead of invading an undefended England? Nazi stupidity was a fact one could count on. But it would be a pity if they did not invade England. If they did not, they would not exhaust all of the inherent possibilities in the war game. It was also a pity because one was obliged to carry on living physically. However, this meant hope for the living animal. These doubts made it exceedingly difficult for one to master the game of groundless life. One had to emigrate to entirely exotic and fantastic lands where we would automatically be shadows; to lands entirely outside of reality; to Thailand or Brazil, for example. Of course, it must be said that the decision to emigrate was partially motivated by the fear of the death of another, but only partially. The real motive was to definitively abandon reality.

§ The relation between space and time, between geography and history, is impenetrably complex. For example, this book, which is a trip into the past, is a search for the future. It attests that both the past and the future are present, because the act of writing this book is not motion in space. Time runs (directionless) within immobile space. Thus, the trip from England to Brazil in 1940, as it emerges within the flux of one's memory today, passes through the unarticulated space of the Atlantic Ocean, on which time stands still. When one stepped onto Brazilian shores, one did not find new space, but new time – or, at least different time, because one had already learned from Kant that time and space are nothing but forms of perception not "realities." However, the experience of stepping off the boat, of being thrown by the waves of the absurd onto the beaches of the unreal, injected an existential dimension into Kantian theories.

§ The same sky shelters Prague and São Paulo. Both cities are immersed in the same space, which is impregnated by the same war. However, in São Paulo the spirit of a different time was blowing. The news of our father's execution awaited in the port of Rio de Janeiro and in Prague mass deportations had begun. In São Paulo the first preparations for an imminent industrialisation born out of the profits of war had started. Prague's agony coincided with São Paulo's puberty: a clash of different times. However, these were nothing but forms of perception, not realities. Only those who were immersed in one of these times could experience the clash. One who hovers above time, who is groundless, can interpret the apparent clash as a form of interchangeable perceptions. By superimposing both senses of time, São Paulo's development seemed like agony and the events in Prague seemed like symptoms of a radically new future. This game of interchanging categories was highly entertaining, but one had to play it alone.

§ This game allowed simultaneous interpretations: the industrialisation of São Paulo was the awakening of the giant in a splendid cradle[1], and the splendidness of the cradle meant the burial of the sweetness in Brazilian life. Prague's agony was the suicide of an anachronism giving way to a new type of world. Prague was the future of São Paulo. And São Paulo was Prague's dream – a dream turned nightmare. The armoured Nazi tanks on the frozen tundra killed the banana trees in São Paulo because they caused industry to emerge there. And this industry would produce more armoured cars, which would kill other banana trees, including the ones we had been dreaming of in Prague. To call the events in Prague "agony" and the ones in São Paulo "birth" is to assume interchangeable points of view. Agony and birth are synonyms for whoever is outside of time. One's arrival in São Paulo was

1. This is a reference to the Brazilian national anthem.

Vilém Flusser

proof that one was an ambassador of armoured cars among banana trees. In other words: one was the cause of "progress," which is synonymous with a microbe carrying a deadly disease called "Prague" – which in turn is a life-endowing disease. That was how one stepped off the boat.

§ This pathologically clear awareness meant that one had to do business during the day and philosophise in the evenings – both from a distance and with nausea. Business at a distance: the aim was to play a game, because profit (and social progress even less) was not the aim. Business with nausea: because of one's awareness of the indignity of what was being done. Philosophy at a distance: because one did not philosophise as in Prague, seeking to absorb ideas to change life. Now one played with ideas. And philosophy with nausea: because of one's awareness of the indignity of what was being done. This double game between business and philosophy – housing profits and gas chambers, import business and Schopenhauer, São Paulo and Prague – was only possible because it was based upon a more fundamental game of love and suicide. One always played with the idea of suicide. And playing with suicide allows for the diabolical freedom of playing between time and with time.

§ This was a solitary game that allowed no partners. Any contact with other immigrants had to be minimal. They threw themselves anxiously into easy business forgetting the war and thinking of

Brazil as a temporary stopover. One did not see the war as real, however, or Brazil as even a temporary stopover, but as another unreality. The reason why other immigrants made one nauseous was this: they did not accept all of this unreality as real. They profited from the war they cried about and thought of as real. And they plundered Brazil, thinking that they were contributing to its "progress," despite not accepting Brazil as a reality. Later, one's distance from other immigrants allowed one an opening to Brazil, and later still, the arduous decision to cut one's new roots. These were two problems that other immigrants would never have. However, this distance immediately generated the following problem: if one behaved like the other immigrants (like the Brazilian bourgeoisie), one hated oneself. And if one behaved differently from them, one became distant from both the other immigrants and the Brazilian bourgeoisie, which reinforced the game with the idea of suicide. This was the existential climate of the first years in São Paulo: the Nazi ovens in the distance, suicide ahead, business during the day, and philosophy in the evenings.

§ Philosophy was all enveloping, but business brought the first contacts with the Brazilian bourgeoisie. Then the discovery: they were groundless. Brothers perhaps? Wrong. In reality: rootless people, not for having lost their roots, but because they never had them. Therefore, a people that did not see itself as groundless, but as the *avant-garde* of a new society. They engaged in business, unaware of what they were doing (even less so than the immigrants). The abyss above, which they hovered, penetrated their bones, but not their wide-eyed awareness. The abyss was covered with thick layers of ideology and empty phrases. They were players, and this is a symptom of any type of groundless existence. However, they were players in a game of luck, not a game of life and death. They were estate agents – not Paschalian. That was one's first image of São Paulo.

§ One saw São Paulo as a mass of groundless people that covered a tenuous nucleus of "real *paulistas*"; a gradually disappearing nucleus. São Paulo was a country town (although it had the same number of inhabitants as Prague), and a ghost town. And it was filled with a collection of trash that had been blown there from all over the world and from the Brazilian countryside. We were also an authentic part of this trash. One was aware of this, but the others were not. They saw themselves as "*bandeirantes*" [explorers]. São Paulo: a place of eternal spring that shimmered with the greening of decomposition and the yellow of pus – and in this sense, a city of the future with capitalism like that of the 19th century and the draining of resources due to patriotic zeal. One could not sustain an honest dialogue with such an environment. One had lost all illusion and ideology, and found oneself in an environment that was saturated with the most fantastic illusions and exotic ideologies. Until one discovered the following: Prague had seemed like a mystical type of dialectic, but eventually revealed itself as a heap of mean serpents. São Paulo initially presented itself as a heap of fantastic alienation, but eventually revealed itself as a place of human decency. This discovery came much later, however, and provoked an unhappy love for São Paulo; an unhappy engagement, which is the aim of this book.

§ The most obvious barrier between São Paulo and us was the war. The newspapers, radio, and consequently every type of small talk revolved around the war. Small talk provoked in us a state of delirium: which war were they talking about? Brazilians were not conscious of the deceitful, kitsch vulgarity of the Nazis, of their ridiculously *petit bourgeois* behaviour, and of the mechanised massification of Germany (phenomena that characterised the brutal cretinism of the war). Brazilians saw a kind of mystical power sweeping across the Old World, and either favoured or (in the majority of cases) stood against the eruption of such "profundities." In other words: Brazilians saw the Nietzschean superman precisely where one saw the Nietzschean herd. It took a long time until one identified this misunderstanding. But when one discovered it, this became extremely fruitful for future communication.

§ The Brazilians who took a position against what was called "Nazism" (against such "profound" power) were exactly the same *petit bourgeoisie* who in Europe sympathised with Nazism. One never had contact with them. The ones who were enthusiastic about "profound Nazism" were of two types: the authentic fascists (*integralistas*) – or in other words, *petit bourgeois* dressed in costumes – and the ones who saw "Nazism" as representing an anti-massifying tendency in Europe. In Europe, this second type would have been on the extreme left fighting in the Resistance. Among the second group there were (and still are) the best elements of the Brazilian intelligentsia, and they were one's future friends. It was tragic that one never managed to explain these misunderstandings to one's own friends, which would have partially explained one's attitudes at the time.

§ Despite the *UFA* films, the American propaganda, and various Brazilian ideologies that deformed reality (if indeed the war had any reality), there were several more-or-less "objective" facts that stood out. The paranoid Nazi attack against the USSR and the megalomaniacal Nazi provocations against the United States sealed the fate of the war and sped up its conclusion. On the other hand, the Nazis had kept their word and were mechanically and efficiently killing the Jews. Did this not represent an obligation to defend a position within an alienated environment? No, one was not obliged. One had already experientially absorbed the mass murders by escaping, and the reports that arrived caused only sensational interest. From one's own perspective, the post-war world that was beginning to be sketched out meant nothing, either externally or internally.

The empty and demagogic phrases of the Atlantic Charter and the Yalta Conference could not disguise that this emerging world would be caught in a conflict between the USSR and the United States. Externally, this was meaningless, because one was geographically and existentially relegated to the world's periphery. Internally, this was also meaningless, because one had lost all hope that a possible revolutionary victory would bring about a new Man. But one still believed that a possible American victory would only confirm the tendency towards barbarous massification. Hence, one was indifferent to the outcome of the war (similarly indifferent to whatever else was upon the stage of current events). The generalised joy in relation to the imminent Nazi defeat was summarily comical: the Nazis had fully realised their role. They had opened the way to a general progress towards totalizing idiotisation. Luckily, however, one had nothing to do with it. One no longer wanted to change the world, but to play at a distance.

§ This is why one delved into philosophy. The Brazilian reality was not disturbing; it was ontologically and aesthetically concealed. Ontologically, all the pompously ridiculous talk concealed the scene. How could one have revealed the patiently passive, suffering *caboclo*, who was cynically manipulated by international interests and the national bourgeoisie, hidden under the *pracinha* who threw himself, burning with ire, into Italian battles that meant nothing to him?

Vilém Flusser

And aesthetically, the scene was concealed by
the unbearable ugliness of São Paulo's urban
environment and the curious fact (never properly
analysed) that everything in Brazil – apparently so
large, empty, and new – was actually small, full,
and old. This meant that Brazilian reality remained
beyond one's existential horizon and did not enter
philosophy. One was in Brazil as if one were on
Mars; contemplating from such groundlessness the
various philosophical systems as if they were ants.
And this type of contemplation resulted in a desire
to sketch a groundless life.

PLAYING WITH SUICIDE AND THE EAST

§ To play with philosophy means to read philosophers – not with the intention of acquiring "criteria," "knowledge," or "values," but to discover the thematic and structural similarities between apparently contradictory philosophies, and to have fun with this. There are at least three ways to philosophise. The first is "academic" and seeks to diligently analyse philosophical texts to discover their messages. This is, generally speaking, how the specialists, philosophy teachers, and universities philosophise. This is a method that can be taught and learned. In Prague, one had already developed an antipathy towards this method because one felt it falsified the essence of philosophy. This antipathy made it difficult to learn the art of philosophy in Prague and served as an explanation why, in São Paulo, one did not try to connect with the universities. Simultaneously, one knew that this method is indispensable for the progress of a disciplined philosophical dialogue. One hoped, however, long before the invention of computers, that thinking machines could fulfil such a task. One of the explanations for this antipathy was psychological: one's father was a philosophy teacher and philosophised in the academic way. Much later, the same antipathy had negative effects in one's struggles with Brazilian philosophy teachers.

§ The second way to philosophise is "from within," and could be described like this: one starts from some ground in which one is rooted and inhabits. This ground is a conscious faith (in Prague this ground had been Marxism). However, conscious faith hides several unconscious layers that vibrate in the ground, and which sustain and endanger it. One sets out from this ground and penetrates philosophy because one doubts the ground. Therefore: one does not enter philosophy in order to consolidate the ground (to "prove" it) but to submit it to being "proven." And there are two important factors. The first is that there is no authentic philosophy that has not sprung from doubt: any philosophical apologia (be it religious or of another ideological form) falsifies philosophy. In this sense, any authentic philosophy is unprejudiced. The second factor is that any doubt presupposes a ground from which one can doubt. Therefore, it presupposes that to philosophise "from within" is prejudiced, however, negatively so. In other words: this type of philosophy advances against the ground it emerges from, in the tacit hope not to destroy but enrich it. As far as this philosophy manages not to inject hope into the philosophical act, but manages "to put hope within inverted commas," it becomes authentic philosophy.

§ The third way to philosophise is "from above," and this way is unprejudiced in a far more radical sense of the term. It doubts nothing because it does not accept anything to be doubted. This method lacks dubious grounding (for example, Descartes and Husserl are seen as naive by this way of philosophising because this method does not see itself as the "thinking thing," or even as being part of a *Lebenswelt* that could be analysed). This philosophy doubts nothing. But the doubts of others are the pawns of its game. Philosophical problems are then seen as chess-like problems – only more fun, since they are better at hiding their ludic character. That was how one philosophised in São Paulo. The philosophers were nothing but pawns in one's philosophy board game.

§ The pawn repertoire was limited, due to the situation in São Paulo during the war. European Continental philosophy did not reach us, so one was limited to Anglo-Saxon philosophy and that of German immigrants. This meant: Cassirer and the Neo-Kantians, Dewey and the Pragmatists, Russell, Whitehead and the Logicians, the Vienna Circle in the United States, some Neo-Hegelians, and a curious type of Marxism (the future "New Left"). One played with them until the gigantic figure of the *Tractatus* overshadowed the scene.

§ One recognised with both fear and happiness a comrade in Wittgenstein. But still, a comrade that belonged to the preceding generation, and therefore, a comrade with different problems. He was like a brother to Kafka and the *Tractatus* was a complement to *The Trial*. Suddenly, it became obvious that Wittgenstein and Kafka imperiously demanded an answer. To understand this, one had to formulate what they were saying at that moment. Essentially, they violently reformulated the Kantian problem of the relation between pure and practical reason. They stated that pure reason is an absurd closed system, which spins on a fixed point around an axis, apparently expanding, but in reality, constantly returning to itself. And they stated that practical reason is entirely inaccessible to pure reason, that, it cannot be analysed; that "life" consists of incomprehensible, inexplicable, and unthinkable lived experiences, which consequently, are meaningless. For Wittgenstein, this was articulated through the statement that pure thought always results in a contradiction or tautology, and that it is necessary to be silent in relation to "facts." In other words: to think, read, write, and speak are escapes towards nothingness. Wittgenstein was a radical positivist: he denied the possibility of thinking anything positive. For Kafka, the same was articulated through the statement that to think is to sin because thought spins on an infernal wheel that does not touch reality; a wheel that grinds us with its unthinking stupidity. In other words: any attempt to orient ourselves within reality (an effort to which we are condemned by the plague of being able to think) necessarily ends in despair. Kierkegaard's crushing God appears in Wittgenstein and Kafka as a chaotic and cretinous *Dasein* (Being-so), as an incomprehensible and unthinkable mechanism – therefore, absurd. To will to believe, know, or valorise, before such cretinism is in itself cretinous. In sum, two bright sentences shed light upon the despairing São Paulo night — Wittgenstein's, "It is not *how* things are in the world that is mystical, but *that* they exist."[2] And Kafka's, "I have spent all my life resisting the desire to end it."[3]

2. From the **Tractatus Logico-Philosophicus**. Routledge & Kegan Paul first published this translation 1961. The revised edition was published in 1974.

3. From **Letters to Milena**, first published in English by Schocken Books in 1952.

§ This demanded an answer, simply for the fact that, absurdly, one had not yet committed suicide. One could play with other philosophers because what they said was merely foolish. With Wittgenstein, however, one could not play. He allowed only two possible answers: to commit suicide or to kill thought. The first answer would have solved the Wittgensteinian problem in a Wittgensteinian manner: problems are resolved if they disappear. The second answer opened up the possibility of reconquering reality, since it had become clear that reality had disappeared due to thought. If one managed to kill thought, one would have managed to live again. *To live*: to stop thinking — that was clear. But is there a method of killing thought?

§ At this point it is necessary to make a confession: the journey into the past is always resisted by our memory, which impedes progress. The memory refuses to reveal everything it hides, and frequently falls silent. Thus, this resistance can be experienced in the effort towards honesty. But in this case, the resistance of one's memory is another issue: it does not fall silent, but provides an ambivalent answer. The question, "Why did one not commit suicide?" has two answers. The first suggests that it was due to cowardice because one feared the pains of death, and the dirtiness of being a disgusting object. The other suggests that it was due to courage because one obscurely believed one still had a task to accomplish, despite being ignorant of the task. Both answers could be perfectly true, despite being contradictory: the fact that one did not commit suicide, but also did not stop playing with the possibility of one's death. The possibility of committing suicide today and not having to face tomorrow made tomorrow viable on a daily basis. In other words: the possibility of suicide opens the field for an answer to Wittgenstein's challenge.

§ So is there a method for stopping thought and being able to live again? For example, is there a method to stop thinking about suicide? The very formulation of such a question already meant overcoming Wittgenstein and Kafka, because it became clear theoretically that it is possible to separate thinking from living and to become distant from one's own thought, to reify and thingify one's own thought; to be a subject and not the object of one's own thoughts. *To live* could mean: to be the subject of one's own thoughts; to think without becoming engaged in one's own thoughts. This was proof that one had lost grounding in a far more radical sense than Wittgenstein and Kafka (at the time one did not have any knowledge of Camus or of Heidegger's step-backwards, so that one's

discovery of distance felt like an isolated thing).
Here was the problem: how to become distant from
one's own thoughts and live, so to speak, on the
other side of them?

§ Given one's isolation in São Paulo, this seemed
like a new problem. The facts were: one played
with philosophy. Therefore, one kept the desired
distance – but not always. One dreamt of Prague.
The nightmares of Prague invaded awakened nights.
They took on an obsessive quality. For example: "Is
it possible to construct a formal synthesis between
Christianity and Marxism without believing it?"
Or: "Is it possible to create scientific art without
believing in it?" This meant that one's situation
had all the characteristics of a psychopathological
problem, and indeed the problem seemed to invite
the solutions offered by psychopathology (as if
a psychological diagnosis could be the "radical
explanation" of the problem). Therefore, one began
to devour books on psychology. However, one
discovered two curious things: one "objective" the
other "subjective." The objective discovery was that
the psychologisation of the problem resulted in
the falsification of the problem, because it started
precisely from a "psychological reality," which one
had already overcome. In other words: psychological
explanations happened within territories already
exploded by Wittgenstein and Kafka. The
subjective discovery was that the study of books
on psychology drew one's interest away from one's
own problems and towards the problems that the

writers could not resolve – but about which they
desperately argued. Therefore, one automatically
became distant from psychology, taking a position
"above" it. Psychology, like everything else, became
a game. This was not the way forward. One had to
become free from thinking through methods that
were beyond the methods of psychology.

§ This was an important discovery, and still persists
to this day. Psychology does not offer *catharsis*
but only explanations and manipulations, just as
any other science does. One may doubt whether
psychology is a "science" or not in the exact sense
of the term, however, one cannot doubt that
psychology is a science in the sense that it deals
only with phenomena and not with "essences"
(whatever the meaning of such a term). This
discovery re-emerged much later, but in different
contexts, and in the following manner: every
"essential" problem is religious, and psychology
is not competent for that. Whenever it attempts
to become competent, when it seeks to absorb
religious elements (carefully, as in Freud, or
unashamedly, as in Jung), the result is probably bad
psychology – but certainly, bad religiosity. Later
on, this came to explain one's visceral aversion to
Jung and one's sympathy for structural psychology
(such as Piaget's), which is limited to psychology's
strictly scientific competence. Surely, one could not
expect any liberation through psychology, in any
sense of the term. Therefore, one accepted it when
Wittgenstein stated that philosophy

has as much in common with psychology as it does with horticulture.

§ If the problem of "liberation" and of "regaining reality" is placed within the coordinates of "the overcoming of thought," then the suspicion that one was leaving the Western structure started to emerge. And the suspicion that the loss of grounding is a far more radical situation than one had believed also started to emerge. The "loss of grounding" seemed to be the loss of the models for experience, knowledge, and values one had in Prague. Now this also seems to be the loss of the structure that organises these models, hence, the loss of the Western structure in the following manner: the tacit presupposition of the Western tradition is that "Being" (irrespective of what that means) is real, positive, and sheltering. And that "Non-Being," is the annihilating danger that surrounds "Being" on all sides. Within such a structure, any salvation (be it Jewish, Christian, Marxist, or any other) means to place oneself in the bosom of Being, sheltered from Non-Being (for example: in God, History, or Idea). Non-Being means Hell. Alas, Wittgenstein and Kafka define thought as "Non-Being" and remain Western. If they want to liberate themselves from thought, it means they want to be free from Hell. However, one's own problem is different. One accepted thought as "Being" and wished to be sheltered in Non-Being. Wittgenstein's answer was to become free from thought in order to commit suicide. Within Western tradition, this was a diabolical answer. But the West was no longer applicable. One had abandoned it. In the lack of grounding, one had overcome both East and West. Therefore, Eastern tradition was a possible option.

§ A word of caution: the trend amongst American and European youth towards the East (which one only became aware of much later) had nothing to do with one's own inclination towards the East. Their aim towards salvation through Eastern cultures was entirely different from one's own. Also, the many wanderings towards the East at the time (Otto, Jung, Eliade etc.) had no bearing on one's decision. These wanderings were, in a certain way, equally suicidal, but they still sought "salvation within Being" – although this was a negative Being. One's decision resulted from a belief that the Western dialectic "Being/Non-Being" did not exist in the Eastern structure. The overcoming of thought through Eastern methods emerged as the overcoming of the Western dialectic, so that "suicide" emerged not as annihilation, but as a dissolution that could not be diagnosed as "Non-Being." Therefore, to overcome thought meant precisely no longer being able to distinguish between Being and Non-Being. One accepted it when Rilke stated that our greatest ill is that we know how to distinguish too well, hence, one's will to *no-longer-Be* acquired a new colouring.

§ The East was no longer the polar opposite of the West, but an open structure (like an anachronism), within which the West could be found. The West was then seen as an organ of the East, but an amputated organ. For example: Western science was unknowingly the search for *Maya*; Marxism was unknowingly the construction of *Karma*; Christ was unknowingly in the West an avatar (like Krishna). However, one's own journey was not the only sign of a trend towards reestablishing contact with the East. The crises of science, Marxism, and Christianity were symptoms of this renewed contact. The famous "twilight of the West" meant a return to the East. China re-emerged thanks to the European catastrophe, and one simply joined the flow. One re-established contact with "reality" by entertaining methods for eliminating thought. That was what Schopenhauer wished he could have done. However, this had nothing to do with P. D. Ouspensky, Theosophy, and Anthroposophy, which were despicable attempts to Westernise the East. No, one would have to methodically and consciously abandon the West to become "saved" by the East.

§ The East was interesting simply as a method for transforming thought into an object of non-thought. The so-called "Eastern Philosophy" (a variety of cosmologies, wisdom, and moralities) was not interesting. One always rejected as puerile any attempt to Westernise these speculations (for example, by drawing parallels with Einstein or Freud). One was permanently convinced that Eastern speculation was a type of primitive magic.

The East was preferable to the West not because it knew better, but precisely because it did not know anything; not because it taught better values, but precisely because it taught no values; not because it had more profound faith, but precisely because it did not have faith in anything; not because it had a more perfect concept of reality, but precisely because it had no concept of reality. Eastern texts were to be read with an entirely different spirit than Western texts: not as theories, but as instruction manuals; as salvation techniques, not as ideologies.

§ If read as ideology, Eastern "wisdom" was ridiculously primitive. It was what Marxists call "naive materialism," because it conceives the "spirit" as a type of thin matter, a spectre, and not as a subject to which matter is an object. That was magic, and one had nothing to do with it; one rejected it. However, the beauty of the East was precisely that its methods were self-contained, without ideology. They were practical in the Kantian sense: ideologically inaccessible. One had to practice them without asking why, what for, and how. One had to practice them without talking about it, in a Wittgensteinian sense. There were two obvious aims sought by Eastern methods: the Indian (*Yoga*) and the Far Eastern (*Buddhism*). The first sought to strengthen the Will that makes us think, so as to expel thought with this strengthened Will (*samadhi*). The other sought to kill the Will in order to stop thinking (*satori*). However, both aims essentially coincided. The

Indian one used the Will to leave itself, and self-overcome. The Japanese one used the Will to delve into itself, and self-overcome. This is so because in the East, unlike for Schopenhauer, Nietzsche, and the Pragmatists, the "Will" is not "Being," but a method of self-dissolution. In sum: the East offered complementary methods. The apparent dialectic between India and China was nothing but Westernised deformation.

§ One read Hindu and Japanese authors (the Chinese were not available) for one's own praxis. The positive and negative results of this effort will not be described here because they are extremely shameful. Only the process will be described. After having achieved concentration, as instructed, one meditated in the following manner: one would take any thought and transform it into an article of faith. For example: "Leon Blum is a defender of the proletariat." Afterwards, one would take the opposite thought and transform that into an article of faith. For example: "Leon Blum is a traitor of the proletariat." The important thing was to believe in the content of the thought, without giving it any importance. Afterwards, one would simultaneously believe both articles of faith. That was difficult, but possible. Thus, a hole emerged in one's thought and faith, and one spun within this hole. So much so that one's spinning could also be observed from without. One could see oneself thinking and believing. Then, an entirely unexpected aesthetic effect emerged that put an end to the whole thing.

§ One saw oneself as a clown in the circus of "salvation of the soul." One did not see oneself as the *Sadhu* in dissolution, but as a fakir at the funfair. One did somersaults on the tightrope. Laughed at everything, and was simultaneously nauseated by the same things. It was like seeing oneself masturbate on sacred ground. The following must also be added: after a certain time (two years more or less), these "enlightenments" started to happen at the most inopportune moments. For example, one started to spin into an "enlightened" state at the office while dictating a letter or at the cathedral square while looking for a restaurant. What kind of liberation was this? It was at least as nauseating as a physical suicide, only not as obvious. Existentially, this brought to an end one's experience with the East. One could never again be free from the experience of ridiculousness and nausea in relation to Eastern methods for the salvation of the soul through "enlightened ecstasy."

§ Much later, when one became interested in the East again and turned the East into an "object of interest," one was able to reinterpret past experiences. Now one could see them as typically technical exercises, as phenomena sympathetic with Western engineering and technocracy. Therefore, once transferred to the West, the techniques of Yoga and other disciplines become typically fascistic: technocratic, efficient, and ridiculously kitsch. At the time, this point of view was not viable. However, something was clear: one could not adopt the East. One had to start all over again. If one could not commit suicide, one had to learn to live differently. This was the task: to stop playing with suicide and the East and try another game.

§ One had delved into one's inner spaces by playing with suicide and the East. Now one was projected towards one's external spaces, as a result of the nausea caused by such a game. This violent diastolic process, which followed a contorted systole, caused a distanced interest. One simultaneously acted and observed oneself acting. Heidegger's backward step (which, much later, would occupy one's centre of interest for years) was already (and long before one's systematic reading of Heidegger's texts) the climate of one's life. One constantly transcended and observed oneself "within one's context" at the most ordinary moments. This distanced point of view problematised one's insertion, and was, at the time, diagnosed as groundlessness. In fact: strictly speaking, one was not one's own problem. The problem was one's insertion into the local context. Not in the sense: "How can I be inserted into this context?" But: "Where am I, when I see myself inserted into this context?" Strictly speaking, this was not the problem of orienting oneself in the world in order to engage oneself with it once again. The problem was how to synthesise the contradiction "engagement/distance." This contradiction, and not so much the contradiction oneself/world was the real challenge.

§ At this point it is necessary to confess a curious fact. Here and now (in other words, France, 1973), the "there" and "then" that are re-emerging from memory (in other words, São Paulo, 1945); appear as objects of distanced contemplation. The "Self" of the here and now is distant from the "Self" of São Paulo in 1945 and today's Self sees that "Self" in a distant contradiction to a third "Self" inserted in the context of São Paulo after the war, so that now one sees the problem of that moment within a much wider context. Here and now, the very contradiction "engagement/distance" emerges as an aspect of an already transcended and overcome context, but also as an aspect of a context with which one is in contradiction right here and now. In other words: one found oneself in the contradiction "engagement/distance," but now one finds oneself in contradiction with the contradiction "engagement/distance." This is nothing but speculation, but it is "speculation" in a concretely existential sense – therefore, a Hegelian sense. Thus, today, when one thinks of São Paulo after the war, one becomes para-Hegelian. At the time, when one sought to live in São Paulo after the war, one became para-Kantian. "A lot happened in the gap between Kant and Hegel."

§ One diagnosed the overpowering, violent diastole as "rebirth." However, such a diagnosis was reached by Kantian transcendence. In other words: the violent interest that began to cause one's external space was diagnosed as a violent reaction to the nausea caused by one's inner space, exactly as it happens in any rebirth. That is why "rebirth" is the opposite of "birth." For example: the rebirth of the fifteenth century was a violent reaction to the nausea caused by Scholasticism; the Carolingian rebirth was a violent reaction to the nausea caused by the Byzantine period; and Pre-Socratic philosophy was very likely a rebirth and violent reaction to an already forgotten nausea caused by mystery and magic. Both history and biography are very likely processes in which systolic periods of nausea alternate with diastolic periods of rebirth. Birth, as well as death, is beyond the horizons of these processes. Neither history nor biography has grounding or immanent aim. At that time, which is now the object of our investigation, this meant that neither history nor biography had an aim or grounding, and, the problem of a possible reborn engagement was enveloped by this climate of absurdity. In other words: one approximated Kant to Wittgenstein, not to Hegel, and transcendental logic seemed to point directly towards the *Tractatus*. That was the climate in which one espoused Goethe's imperative "*stirb und werde!*"[4] – that is, as a non-Spinozan categorical imperative. The disenchanted return towards Marxism, via Spinoza, Hegel, and Adorno, was painstakingly happening only then, during one's second phase of distancing. Unfortunately, however, that was only a "rebirth," or "neo-Marxism." And there is nothing more senile and disenchanted than phenomena prefixed by "neo," which is an unforgettable (and insurmountable) teaching provided by "*Neues Deutschland.*"

4. From **Moganni Nameh - Buch des Sängers in West-östlicher Divan** published in 1819 and expanded in 1827.

Groundless

§ The scene that emerged from the opening of one's external spaces was, to a large extent as follows. The war had ended in a completely unexpected climax: the Hiroshima and Nagasaki bombs. The ethical problem raised by this climax gave way to an immediate ontological problem. The ethical problem was this: Jews who had emigrated from Germany and Italy had created the atomic bomb. In other words, these scientists did not see a contradiction between theory and practice because they were engaged in nuclear research through theory and against Nazism, in practice, therefore, both aims coincided. However, the bombs had been dropped on Japan, not on Germany, and not by the scientists, but by the American administration. History demonstrated the latent contradiction between theory and practice. Furthermore, the climax showed that history had shifted from the Atlantic to the Pacific, proving that Prague had been expelled from the centre (as well as that Nazism was an epiphenomenon, which was something that one already knew). Further still: the first bomb, dropped on Hiroshima, was the climax. As such, it was ethically bearable. But the second bomb, the one dropped on Nagasaki, was an unbearable anti-climax. One could not fathom why these three ethical factors (theory/practice, Atlantic/Pacific, and climax/anti-climax) were not the focus of general discussion, but were concealed by an unreal conversation concentrated on "The Marshall Plan."

Vilém Flusser

§ One's own interest was centred on the ontological problem raised by the atomic bomb. From the perspective of theory, the bomb experientially proved the known hypothesis, according to which matter is nothing but concentrated energy and "energy" is synonymous with "the destruction of matter," which means that energy is the internal antithesis of matter. Thus, experientially, the bomb was proof of a radical dialectical materialism: matter contradicts itself. And from a practical perspective, the bomb was experiential proof that humanity had reached a stage of technological progress that allowed for a collective suicide, taking the form of either a duel or *harakiri*. One believed, somewhat innocently, that both the practical and theoretical aspects of the bomb would become the backdrop against which every individual and collective event would unfold. In other words, one believed that the illusion of the material world and the precariousness of history would become the basis for future consciousness. One ridiculously underestimated the human capacity to avoid an issue and forget Nothingness and Death.

§ Consequently, one observed the events of the time and several other types of madness: the reconstruction of Europe, the Cold War between the USSR and the United States, the Asian convulsions, and the pseudo-liberation of Africa. But how could everyone pretend that the atomic bomb did not exist, as if history could return to its rhythm, idiotically interrupted by Hitler? Or was it a collective "putting in parenthesis" of the bomb, so that any political engagement was nothing but make-believe? And what to say of continuing scientific progress? Should one suspend the knowledge of approaching death? Or was "pure" theoretical interest perhaps the reason for scientific progress; to always know better about everything and nothing? On the other hand, one could not think that amidst this madness one was the only one to escape it, as this thought would itself have been sheer madness. The proof of this was in Brazil, in one's immediate circumstance.

§ Everything that was happening in Brazil emerged like a deliberate fiction. The people around us not only suspended their knowledge of the atomic bomb, but also their knowledge of the decisive power that the United States exerted upon Brazil. They pretended to be "building a future." From one's perspective, not only the political, social, and economic discussions, but also the philosophical and cultural ones were bathed in this climate of deliberate refusal to accept the situation. This had an air of collective conspiracy: "let us pretend." And one could not honestly take part in such a conspiracy (even though one had already felt a hint of desire to play the game "what if," because one had began to discover the Brazilian human warmth). Much later, one finally understood the purpose of that "hide-and-seek" game: no one is able to accept his or her own situation as an object of third party manipulation. Whenever real freedom of choice is lacking, a fictitious freedom has to be conjured so that the possibility of becoming a subject may at least exist in fantasy. A fantasy that may, in the long run, structure itself so that it ends up replacing the unbearable and concealed "reality." This fantasy may, in the long run, acquire several "real" characteristics, especially if the fantasy is based upon concrete things such as factories and paintings, thus keeping "reality" concealed and impenetrable.

§ The knowledge of the Brazilian game of "hide-and-seek" came much later, and resulted in one's engagement in all things Brazilian. Because, one finally understood not only that the game was vitally necessary, but that it was also both deliberate and unknowing. One joined the game with heart and soul. And, much later still, one painstakingly understood that our role was to make the game visible to one's game-partners, even though this revelation was dangerous for the game's continuance. The contradiction between one's conviction that the game was vitally necessary and the conviction that one's role was to uncover this, led to the decision to disengage. This came much later. But at that time, which is now under scrutiny, one felt repulsion for the "hide-and-seek" game because one interpreted it as fundamentally dishonest. Therefore, one withdrew from Brazilian culture, but open up to Brazilian nature.

§ The distance caused by writing this book now, sheds a curious light upon the decision taken at that time. The twenty-eight years that separate 1945 from today have seen a radical modification of the human context. Western Europe went from being a potholed battlefield to becoming the first proper bourgeois society in history, with unparalleled material wealth and unequalled decisive power since the First World War. Simultaneously, Eastern Europe has become the cradle for the majority of new cultural and philosophical events of recent times. Contrary to what was expected in 1945, the European "miracle" represents the most important factor in these events. At the same time, America seems to have peaked in power, the USSR seems to have stagnated, the Japanese "miracle" seems less fundamental than it promised, and China's awakening has been a very slow process. The most important thing is that the so-called "Third World," in other words, Southeast Asia, Africa, and Latin America continue to occupy, despite superficial changes, *the-field-for-third-party-decisions*, as well as continuing to be fundamentally culturally and socially sterile. The radical change was the surprising emergence of Europe. But appearances can deceive. Every historical event of the last generation has been bathed in a climate of unreality, as if history advanced by inertia and not from an inherent power. Could the atomic bomb (and its correlations) be the explanation for this, or could the explanation be hidden in deeper layers? In any case, in the light of today's reflection, the decisions

one made then seem far more rational than those
that followed, in favour of an engagement with all
things Brazilian. The previous generation's history
wanted to prove that the view one had of the
world in 1945 was approximately correct, and that
any engagement with history – and, *a fortiori*, with
Brazilian history – was nothing but anachronism.
In the current reflection, the eventual engagement
with Brazil is revealed as the fruit of the illusions
that emanated from the Brazilian environment,
and also from the sympathy that emanated from
that environment, as well as from the feeling of
responsibility for the misery characteristic of large
portions of this environment. However, these are
nothing but recent reflections.

§ At the time, to become integrated with Brazilian
nature meant to grow roots in a non-historical, and
therefore, non-human reality (an eminently different
procedure from one's current attempt to integrate
into European nature). This meant keeping one's
distance from history and culture – in other words,
from "human things" – and reaching for "a more
stable reality," found in the things of nature. This
was undoubtedly a search for solitude, and in this
sense it meant escapism. However, it also meant
the acceptance of a challenge: the hostile wide-
openness of the Brazilian territory. One was in
a country whose population was densely heaped
along its inhumanly long coastline, and whose
almost unpopulated countryside seem to call with
an imperative tone: "Come and take me!" From

one's own perspective, this was not about the conquest of the Western country. This was not "Go West, young man!" not Brasilia, or the Trans-Amazonian Motorway, or even settler culture. This was an invitation to go find one's Self in the wide-openness of nothingness, and not an invitation to become "realised" in this wide-openness (also losing one's Self in the process). Much later, when one became a friend to João Guimarães Rosa, one understood that there were others who also had heard the "call from the mountain." And later still, through exchanges with Dora Ferreira da Silva, one began to understand the religious dimensions of such a calling. One understood then that the calling from this wide-openness meant the full dimension of Brazilian existence, and that Brasilia and the Trans-Amazonian Motorway were from opposite dimensions – J. Kubitschek versus Riobaldo, or immanentist historisation versus transcendentalist existentialisation: these were the two poles, between which, Brazilian existence oscillates.

§ One began to travel through the Brazilian countryside with the excuse of buying and selling things. However, the aim was not to come into contact with the country folk (this was a mere corollary). The aim was to come into contact with Brazilian nature. The result was a total failure. Contrary to what one had hoped, contact with Brazilian nature resulted in an almost pathological alienation; an irrational and strongly emotional denial of such an inhuman wide-openness. Before attempting an analysis of this, it is necessary to confess that the hatred Brazilian nature provoked strongly contributed to one's posterior engagement with Brazilian culture. One associated "Brazilian culture" with the "struggle against Brazilian nature," and more than anything, this aspect of Brazilian culture was highly engaging. By extension, one began to associate "culture *tout court*" with the "struggle against nature *tout court*," including against human nature. This association, which initially was entirely subconscious, became progressively conscious. Finally, it became clear that one's engagement with culture was nothing but a battle against one's own "nature." Once again, this meant another type of suicide. Once this became clear, not only one's engagement with Brazilian culture, but culture in general, fell into crisis.

§ One's contact with nature was a dialectic shock: the meeting of a particular, objective situation with a particular subjectivity. The objective situation (as much as the current distance allows one to see it) is the following: an immense, slightly undulating plain without noticeable faults, covered by relatively low but sporadically dense vegetation, which forms the nucleus of Brazilian nature. The plain inclines to the west towards great swamps, through which most of the rivers run cutting through the plain and falling east towards the ocean in two abrupt elevations, the *Mantiqueira Ridge*, and the *Sea Ridge* where the plain turns its back to the sea and faces the continent. Two colours dominate the plain: a reddish purple soil that tends to rise as dust and the dark green of perennial vegetation. The climate is humid and subtropical on the southern part of the plain and tends to be dry, continental, and tropical the farther north one advances. Atmospheric pressure is consistently high. Hence, the sensation of oppression and depression predominates, interrupted only by clear nights and a few crisp, liberating mornings. The sunlight is very strong and kills all colours, except the brightest ones. Animal life is surprisingly rare, save for insects and reptiles. There are almost no flowers, but there are flowering trees. The impression caused by the plain could be summed up as pacific, sweet, and depressingly senile. Brazilian nature shows itself as a grand old lady who conserves all of her femininity without exerting any sexual allure, or even provoking desire. For whomever seeks to dominate her, this gigantic, grand old lady reveals herself as relatively sterile, strong willed, and very cunning.

§ For those approaching Brazilian nature from Europe, senility and archaism mark the encounter. The land's geologic features are old and worn out, like an elephant's skin. In the botanical kingdom, life forms from the Carboniferous period dominate. The archaism of the palm trees and plants, reminiscent of fossilised plants, evokes the sensation of a remote past. There are reptiles that seem like miniature dinosaurs. Marsupials and toothless species can be found. And since all of this exists under a high-pressure dome in which the sky feels low, the experience of nature is like being in a greenhouse in which bygone geological ages have been preserved.

§ The subjectivity with which one approaches this greenhouse may be outlined in the following way: nature is the exuberant and caring mother who shelters us in her bosom, as well as the fun and exciting lover who wants to be seduced and embraced. This image of nature was profoundly rooted in us consciously (thanks to myths, fairy-tale, and literature) and experientially (thanks to one's contact with European nature). Whenever one said "nature," one imagined light green woods, flowering meadows, snow covered rocks, and sea bays that penetrate the entrails of the continent. Of course, one knew that this was not the type of nature that awaited us in the Brazilian backlands. However, one still nurtured the paradisiacal illusion that the term "tropics" evokes in Europeans. The disillusion was terrible.

§ If the Brazilian countryside had at least been a desert, one could have connected with it. The greatness of the desert (like the greatness of the sea) could have devoured and swallowed one in one's search for oneself. However, the Brazilian backlands was not grandiose. It was an enormous collection of small things. Small valleys surrounded by small hills that hid other small valleys, *ad infinitum*. This was the opposite of greatness; it was tedium. One could go in any direction, traveling for hundreds of kilometres, but would always find the same kind of nature. One resisted succumbing to such an incredible lack of variety until one comprehended that this was precisely what was so terrifying about Brazilian nature: one is ground up and destroyed by its eternally repeating pettiness. The colossal rivers cutting through the countryside are of no value: they are much smaller than the small rivers of Europe because their colossal size lacks perspective. In sum: this is a nature that neither shelters nor induces fright, but grinds us down. One found it impossible to find oneself while living within it.

§ There were other possibilities, of course, such as the *Sea Ridge* and the *Mantiqueira Ridge* or the beaches. For example, Campos do Jordão or Maceió. These "nature" islands, as one called them, persisted like dreams floating perpetually on the horizon of one's mind. If one was honest, however, one had to admit the following: Campos do Jordão was nothing but nostalgia because it represented the closest possible copy of European nature. And Maceió was nothing but fantasy representing the closest possible copy of an "ideological tropic"; of paradise. To be a refugee on these islands, immersed in one's own ideology, would not have meant that one had found oneself, but that one had abandoned oneself. This would have meant defeat. Curiously, one was not ready to accept defeat because one felt more clearly than before that one had a certain nebulous vocation linked to the typewriter and the linguistic articulation of thoughts and dreams. One's search

in nature for rootedness thus began to reveal its
real aim: grounding in order to write in solitude
and become self-realised. Brazilian nature did not
allow this, and that is why it was so odious. And
both of the previously mentioned islands did not
allow it because one had already diagnosed them as
deceitful. This meant one felt rejected by Brazilian
nature as a writer. Hence, one turned towards
Brazilian culture.

§ The experience of attempting to integrate with
Brazilian nature was to colour one's whole future
life. This partially explains one's painful engagement
with all things Brazilian, as well as, one's recent
return to Europe. Although "European reality" had
been revealed as an illusion, one had never stopped
longing for European nature. The Bohemian fields,
the Alps, the Mediterranean beaches, and French
woodlands had always existed as horizons in
everything one did. One's aim was to Europeanise
Brazil, and whenever this became impossible, one's
engagement collapsed.

§ During the last years of the 1940s one began to establish the first authentic contact with Brazilian culture. And it must be said, from the start of this adventure, which would decisively mark the course of one's life, one's attitude in approaching such a culture was an attitude seeking engagement. In other words, one sought to learn and understand the culture as profoundly as possible, not only to absorb and assimilate it to one's own culture, but to act within it as well, thereby marking the lived experience that Brazilian culture causes in us. In general, cultures provide three types of lived experience:

§ (A) The culture to which one belongs at birth, which informs us from the "start" ("start" could mean both the awakening of consciousness and earlier unconscious layers) also informs the environment in which one lives, and is experienced as "given." This culture is both a determining aspect of the environment into which one is thrust at birth, and an aspect of the freedom one has in order to rebel against the environment's limiting aspect. Thus, the vast majority of people experiences this culture as culture *tout court*, and the discovery that it is only one among several existing cultures (among all the available cultures) is attained by only a few people. Effectively, this discovery contains the germ of the groundlessness-malady, because it allows an external view of the culture to which we belong. The ones who truly belong to their cultures do so because they never grasped such a discovery. This was the situation in which one found oneself in Prague. The important thing, in order to understand such a situation, is that it did not exclude information about other cultures. However, these other cultures were not seen as alternatives to our own, but as problems to be dealt with, within the parameters of one's own culture, which structured one's universe – and in this sense, encompassed every other culture. One would not have "discovered" Brazilian culture if one had studied it in Prague. On the contrary, one would have concealed it within Praguean culture (doing what could be termed as "Brazilian culturology" with Praguean cultural methods and categories). But if Brazilian culture had emerged as an alternative to Praguean culture, one would have "existentially" discovered it, in the sense of removing the Praguean cover (perhaps the difference between "discovery" and "knowledge" explains a fundamental problem within anthropology: one may attain a far deeper and more detailed knowledge of Eskimo culture than any Eskimo ever could, but, one would still not have "discovered" such a culture). In this context, the following question emerges: can one "discover" one's own culture, in the sense of "discovering oneself"? Or does one "discover" one's own culture only after abandoning it, that is, after abandoning oneself? This is the problem of "transcendence," and one could not escape Kant now or then.

Vilém Flusser

§ (B) Once one has transcended one's own culture (or, reached a situation of groundlessness), one starts to float above a complex set of cultures – and picture oneself floating. This implies a series of problems, on many levels. For example: one starts to see cultural interpenetrations, hierarchies, and abysses between cultures, as well as the various dynamics that allow them to interpenetrate, become distant, and devour each other. This invites comparison between cultures, but excludes any valorisation and, therefore, any engagement with a particular culture. Another example: one is constantly called upon to give an account of how much the apparently transcended culture remains active within oneself, which means that one is constantly called upon to transcend oneself. By seeing oneself as a "cultural factor" though (one is a "Self" in relation to a particular culture – the one apparently transcended), this constant state of transcendence is equivalent to a constant emptying of one's "Self." Groundlessness thus becomes a constant process of self-alienation, of abandoning one's "Self." This is an aspect of the "suicide game" discussed earlier. Third example: seen from this situation, every culture emerges as a field for engagement – but a field from which one may only take something for one's own profit. One thus becomes a sponge, absorbing elements from any culture (perhaps this is the true meaning of the term cosmopolitan: the universal, passive, and irresponsible ability to profit). This explains one's experience in relation to Eastern culture, and may also explain the nausea it provoked. In this situation, every culture is thus experienced as a more or less structured set of models (a game); an experience to which Nietzsche came close in his *Zarathustra*. This is possibly a type of "supra-human" experience, but certainly inhuman and dehumanising.

§ (C) One may find oneself on the border between two clashing cultures, which is the situation of the classic immigrant type (this was not the case in Prague, because the three fundamental cultures, Czech, German, and Jewish, formed a synthesis and therefore a new culture). Emigration takes one all the way to the border of one's culture (it allows one to experience the limits of the culture), and immigration takes one all the way to the border of another culture (it allows one to experience the other culture from the inside out). The immigrant's task is defined by the situation in which he finds himself: he must seek to synthesise both cultures within himself, and then seek to progressively encourage the "new" culture to replace the "old" culture in his "form" of *being-in-the-world*. The dialectic process through which the immigrant absorbs the new culture, and is absorbed by it, does not pose a problem of engagement. To put it simply, one "reality" gradually replaces the other and the abyss of groundlessness is never revealed (of course, the dialectic process varies according to culture: this variation will be discussed later). This process of replacement of one culture by another is slow; it happens mainly in unconscious layers and it generally covers a larger span of time than the immigrant's own life. The immigrant transfers the assimilation process to his children, and even his grandchildren, and it is impossible to fully verify a clear passage from one culture to another at any given point. The problem of engaging with the "new culture" does not emerge because one imperceptibly slides towards it. The "new culture" is experienced as the progressive penetration into a new reality. One had never gone through such an experience, and that set one apart from the other immigrants with whom one had contact. During the first ten years of life in Brazil, that country's culture was one amongst many observed from the distance of one's own groundlessness. However, suddenly one decided (*Entschluss*) to become engaged, which meant, that one's experience of this culture was not framed within any of the types of experience previously sketched out here. This partly explains the curious fact that, from then on, one felt a lot more connected to "native Brazilians" than to other immigrants.

§ Since how one experiences a language is a fundamental aspect of how one experiences a culture, attempting a phenomenological description of how one experienced Brazilian culture, after deciding to engage with it, is made easier by the fact that this culture emerged more clearly in the form of the Brazilian language. In the type of experience (A), one's language is experienced as "language *tout court*" and every other language is seen as an object-language and one's language becomes a meta-language. In other words, the native language serves as a tool for the study and domination of other languages. In the type of experience (B), every language is observed from an extra-linguistic position (for example, from structural analysis), which is the Wittgensteinian position (this is why one always felt a similarity between the Wittgensteinian and Nietzschean positions). In the type of experience (C), the "new" language is experienced as a communication medium with the new environment and imperceptibly starts to displace one's native language, gradually becoming "one's language." The classic immigrant in Brazil gradually learns Portuguese to be able to communicate with Brazilians and, imperceptibly becomes dominated by Portuguese, which starts to structure one's thoughts, consequently, one's grasp of the world. However, one's experience of the Portuguese language was entirely different from theirs.

§ The decision to engage with Brazilian culture was fundamentally a decision in favour of engaging with the Brazilian language. This meant one did not absorb the language in order to use it for daily contact with Brazilians, but as a tool for expression. In other words, Brazilian Portuguese was not experienced as the language spoken in Brazil, but as the raw material with which one was going to work in order to realise one's life. One experienced the language as a challenge and as a life project. Thus, the characteristic dialectic between the subject that seeks to inform matter and the matter to be worked upon was established from the start. The epistemological aspect of this dialectic was that one sought to penetrate the essence of the Portuguese language in order to modify it from within, and simultaneously be penetrated by that essence in order to be modified by it. The emotional aspect of this dialectic was that one became enamoured with the Portuguese language, imbued by its beauty, but at the same time, one began to passionately hate the language as it gradually resisted one's efforts to modify it. The existential aspect of this dialectic was that one began to live according to the Portuguese language, which became the field of one's engagement. But at the same time, one started to use the language as a tool, or as a medium for engaging with a supra-linguistic reality (Brazilian society). To sum up this dialectic: one sought to be dominated by Portuguese in order to dominate it, and to engage with Brazilian society. The synthesis of this dialectic, the aim of this engagement, was to become a Brazilian writer.

§ By deciding to engage, the situation in which one found oneself was the following: one had a relatively complex bilingual education; during infancy one spoke Czech, although German was never a foreign language. One's primary schooling was in German, but the majority of one's contact with the surroundings continued to be in Czech.

One's secondary schooling was in German, and during that period German was the dominant language. Maturity was reached through German, but then quickly repeated in Czech. The few academic semesters one enjoyed were in the Czech university. When we abandoned Prague, one was impregnated with the German language on every level except the most concrete one, which was dominated by Czech. However, the dominance exerted by the German language was problematised by two factors: the constant infiltration of Czech structures, and the aesthetic rejection one felt towards German as used by the Nazis. One was passionately in love with the German language as it was formulated deep within us (for example, through Schiller, Nietzsche, Rilke, and Kafka), but one simultaneously loved the Czech language as the founding structure of one's concrete thought. Therefore, one's engagement with writing in Prague had very clear coordinates: write in German in order to enrich it with Czech structures, and therefore resist its vulgarisation by the Nazis; write in order to save German with Praguean injections. One must note that the German language, in its written form today, seems upon one's return to Europe, as the most sorrowful victim of Nazism.

§ The Prague schools had given us a relatively solid "classical" education, which meant solid knowledge of Latin structure, and some familiarity with Greek structure. Latin never became a language in the fullest sense of the term, but its syntax (the delightful play with rigid forms in order to reach exact and simultaneously "open" meanings) invaded one's German. Latin became one's stylistic model for writing in German. Greek worked in the opposite way: its agglutinating capacity, the way it forms *porte-manteaux*, reinforced and ennobled a similar tendency in German, as well as encouraged us to create neologisms. This agglutinative similarity between Greek and German explains the "Hellenism" of so many German philosophers and poets and why they manage to penetrate Greek thought. *"Das Land der Griechen mit der Seele suchend"* (One searches for the land of the Greeks through the soul), could be translated as "one searches for the thought of the Greeks through similar German grammatical forms." This meant that one's engagement with writing implied not only introducing Czech structures into German, but also Latin ones and a hint of Greek forms.

§ One's engagement with Zionism during the last years in Prague provided a minor knowledge of Hebrew, which turned out to be a violent revelation. It was curious to observe that, during the Hebrew lessons, one was the only person to undergo such a shock. Hebrew revealed itself to be an entirely different thought structure (meaning created through a game with verb roots and a virtually non-existent present tense) and a radically different, new way of relating to the world (*Sachverhalte*), due to the absence of the verb "to be" and the existence of the term *"yesh,"* which is generally translated – badly –

as "there is." Hebrew emanated an aura of archaism and sacredness, despite its deliberate modernisation by the Zionists. This created a challenge, which, unfortunately, one never fully adopted, due to a lack of time. However, Hebrew´s inherent, transcendent form of signification lingers to this day.

§ During the last years in Prague, one read Ortega y Gasset. His style was far more fascinating than his message: a simple, economic, and penetrating type of writing. One had always considered the aphorism the appropriate style for *being-in-the-world*, which is why Heine (a noble, and unfortunately rare brand of journalism) and Nietzsche (not so much a violation of language but a violation of thought through language) emerged as ideals to be followed. Curiously, Marx, with his violent dialectic game of opposing terms, had been aesthetically repellent – but intellectually attractive. With Ortega y Gasset, however, one found a master: irony without cynicism and stylistic economy without double-entendre. For this reason, one studied Spanish (not in order to emigrate, as others did). Spanish was not the language of Buenos Aires or Bogotá (or of Rio de Janeiro as was commonly thought in Prague) but the language of Ortega y Gasset. Once again, however, Hitler arrived too early, curtailing any concrete results that could have come from studying Spanish. What one wrote in Prague was a kind of blind search for Ortega y Gasset.

§ The escape to England cut short one's existential ties with the German language, but it opened the wide horizons of the English language. Perhaps due to one's groundlessness, this incredible language penetrated with surprising ease. On a colloquial level, English is unequalled in its syntactic poverty and simplicity. On the technical and scientific levels, however, it is unparalleled in its rigour and economy. On the philosophical and literary levels, English is unparalleled in its complexity and profundity. On the level of poetic beauty, it is almost unbearable. English is the language of all languages. But this all lies buried to "continental" ears behind its strange repulsive, sounding melody. Although theoretically Germanic, like the German language, English is, in a sense, the opposite of German. English tends to be monosyllabic, whereas German leans towards agglutination. Syllables like "put," which are meaningful only within context, distance English entirely from Greek but move it close towards Chinese. Of course, in such a situation, one was obliged to stop writing entirely and wait until English was better absorbed. This absorption continued in Brazil, where one read books almost exclusively in English. Two stylistic models began to emerge: that of B. Russell and E. Pound and that of J. Dewey and H. Melville. And the following problem emerged: should one write in German, but absorbing English, or in English absorbing German, along with all the implications clinging to it since Prague? The search for Brazilian nature was essentially a search for grounding in order to resolve this problem. In sum: one was in the "B" situation in relation to these languages; one hovered above them.

§ It is curious, in retrospect, that the Portuguese language did not emerge as a challenge during the first years in Brazil. One had learned this language with great ease (thanks to Latin, a more or less superficial knowledge of French, Italian, and Spanish — and especially, due to one's groundlessness). But one used it only for daily communication. One spoke it reasonably well but had not delved into its structure or into the fascinating essence hidden within it. Later, this blind attitude towards Portuguese would complicate one's engagement with it. One eventually had to relearn the language — an arduous task since it meant having to forget what one had already learned. A characteristic feature of one's engagement was that one never fully managed to eliminate one's "first" Portuguese. One's love for the Portuguese language thus persisted as an unhappy love, even though it produced some texts that are not bad. In other words: German, and even English, were always — and even today — the languages in which one wrote with greatest ease. The consequence of this is that Portuguese is still one's true task, precisely because it is the most difficult.

§ In sum, the situation in which one gradually opened up to Portuguese was this: it became the language to be absorbed, manipulated by one's

Czech, Latin, Greek, and Hebrew-infected-German,
as well as by one's English – having Ortega y Gasset
as a stylistic model. The task of a lifetime. Life
began anew.

§ Viewed as raw material, the Portuguese language
demands very different techniques of manipulation
from the ones demanded by German and English.
This discovery, which emerged right at the
beginning of one's engagement with Portuguese,
influenced much later the long discussions one had
with J. Guimarães Rosa on the phenomenology of
spoken and written Portuguese, through critiques
aimed at the Concrete poets – especially Haroldo
de Campos – and through one's own review of
Dora Ferreira da Silva's translations of R. M. Rilke.
The situation might be illustrated in the following
manner: German and English are like vertebrates
in which rules function like a skeleton supporting
a growing organism, whereas Portuguese rules
function like a shell growing in layers to protect the
organism. This image allows several conclusions that
are valid, to a certain point.

§ (I) The English skeleton is far simpler and more
deliberate than the German one. Consequently,
the syntactic challenge offered by the English
language is more restricted: its syntax is almost
perfect. German syntax, conversely, allows richer
manipulations with surprising effects – but without
breaking the skeleton. In other words: in German
one can perform a kind of gymnastics that contorts

its limbs into bizarre positions without breaking its bones. In Portuguese, however, the situation is entirely different because its syntax is far more consistent than German and far more complex than English. This presents a challenge for anyone who manipulates Portuguese syntax, because it breaks easily. Lying hidden within the Portuguese lexicon's soft matter are hard, shiny, opaque pearls ("sayings" as Mário Chamie calls them) that shine through the cracks and appear in layers of the shell. What this means is that, when E. E. Cummings does "concrete poetry" and J. Joyce plays with basic elements of language, English syntax remains intact, and when C. Morgenstern does "concrete poetry" and T. Mann plays with basic elements of German, the syntax is violated but its rules are preserved. But when Pedro Xisto does "concrete poetry" and J. Guimarães Rosa plays with basic elements of Portuguese, the shell of its syntax cracks; its rules are broken and its hidden essence emerges. One could say that the Brazilian Concretists' interest in Russian "Modernists," especially Mayakovski and Yesenin, is perfectly justified: the Russian language probably has more meaningful similarities with Portuguese than several other languages.

§ (2) The English organism grows almost freely, supported by its skeleton, although the skeleton remains untouched. Consequently, almost every foreign component can be easily anglicised; every neologism is quickly absorbed – or not even experienced as a neologism. The German organism grows with more difficulty, since the skeleton that supports it must adapt to growth. Consequently, the Germanisation of foreign components is a creative challenge because several neologisms created in this manner have demanded a manipulation of the German syntax. Also, since German has a great capacity for creating "internal" neologisms (thanks to its agglutinating tendency), the introduction of foreign elements is a dangerous task. However, the Portuguese organism cannot grow without breaking the rules enveloping it. Consequently, the introduction of foreign elements means the liberation of that language and engagement against Portuguese syntax. Neologisms constantly infiltrate the Portuguese language, and they come from somewhat exotic contexts, for example, Bantu, Guarani, Japanese, and Yiddish: which means the emergence of a dangerous dialectic between the enrichment of language and the loss of its identity. This dialectic is powerful and may be described thus: the Portuguese language, all of it, is put into question every time that it is manipulated.

§ (3) The near perfection of English syntax tends to make it invisible, just as the perfect apparatus becomes invisible, which creates the illusion of freedom. In other words: apparently everything is allowed in English, precisely because in reality everything is almost perfectly organised. To subvert the English language means, therefore, to reveal its hidden rules. The syntactic studies of English, while subversive, are highly creative. This partially explains the success of the Prague School and the Vienna Circle in England and the U.S.A. The complexity, inconsistency, and flexibility of German syntax, which are responsible for the "depth," obscurity, and lack of logic in German thought open up a wide field for discoveries. To reveal German syntax could mean to reveal "deep" layers; Heidegger's analyses of a few sentences by Hölderlin and Nietzsche prove it. However, in Portuguese, syntax is on the language's surface. Consequently, analyses of Portuguese syntax, which abound, are academic, formal, and lacking in interest. The real engagement Portuguese demands is to drive against its syntax in favour of hidden semantic treasures. One could elaborate on this even further. But to sum it all up: to write in English and German means to manipulate the semantic layer in order to reveal the syntax. To write in Portuguese means to break the syntax in order to reveal the hidden semantic secrets. This could be further generalised: to become engaged with Brazilian culture means to break the formalist shells (Positivism, Marxism, etc.) in order to reveal hidden semantic secrets (for example, its mysticism and messianism). In this sense, Euclides da Cunha remains to this day an unachievable model.

§ Additionally, a fundamental consideration must be made in relation to written language. English and German orthography are more etymological than phonetic, which means that to read in these languages is to discover their past. However,

Portuguese orthography superbly rejects etymology and seeks perfect phonetic spellings. To read in Portuguese is an exercise in ahistoricity. For example, the shock of having to write "*ciência*" [science], without the "s" and with the "^", was an unforgettable experience. These spelling "mistakes" revolutionise their languages, since orthography can only be modified with great difficulty. In Portuguese, these "mistakes" are not so meaningful. Portuguese orthography changes constantly through academic convention (almost diplomatic) and adapts to the flow of pronunciation in different contexts. Therefore, the challenge for whoever writes in Portuguese is not orthography but pagination. And the visual aspect of Portuguese is not manipulable through letters within words but by the modification of words within sentences. From this standpoint, a curious parallel could be drawn between Portuguese and Russian.

§ Obviously, in every Western language, to write does not mean merely to arrange letters on a surface but also to transcribe spoken language, no matter whether its orthography is phonetic or not. This means, in other words, not only to create drawings but also to compose musically. Neither English nor German are terribly melodic, and this is their greatest challenge. Harmony dominates German and rhythm English. This partially explains why great English writers favour melody, as in Pound's *The Cantos*, Elliot's great melodies, and Shakespeare's *Sonnets*. This also explains partially the unequalled

Romantic German songs and *Duino Elegies*. However, Portuguese is a melodic language *par excellence*; when speaking it one is almost singing. Hence, melody is not a challenge and the Portuguese and Brazilian Romantics are sweet to the point of being indigestible. The real challenge in Portuguese is harmony (Cassiano Ricardo is an example), but especially rhythm. Unbelievably, this challenge was not detected until the emergence of Bossa Nova. In a country where African rhythm dominates every field – which in a certain way permeates the culture as a whole – literary and poetic production was limited to a mechanical calculation of syllables that was entirely alienated from reality. This is why Bossa Nova represents an aesthetic revolution of the first order, far more than the famous week of 1922 – not so much as music, but as literature. Bossa Nova is the first conscious manipulation of Portuguese rhythm.

§ At this point, one must clear a few misunderstandings, all of which are related to the transposition of foreign literature to Brazilian soil. The new American, English, German, and French novels are not as productive in Brazil as they are in their original countries because they do not grasp the essence of the Portuguese language. The great writers, such as Clarice Lispector, are fully aware of this and pursue different paths. Guimarães Rosa is not a Brazilian J. Joyce. There is no sense in transposing Norman Mailer when he is engaged in the discovery of English syntax. On the other pole

lies the problem of translating Saint-John Perse
and R. M. Rilke. Their positions, in their respective
contexts, are ambivalent. They are engaged with
melody and in this sense they are revolutionary
and subversive. However, they do not battle the
discourse of their languages, and in this sense they
are decadent. They represent the apex of a moment
in transition. But in the Portuguese language
context, their ambivalence disappears – except for
Dora Ferreira da Silva's translations, which add
a harmonic dimension that is missing from the
original texts. This raises the issue, however, of
the "freedom of translation," which will be dealt
with later in this book. Even more importantly,
linguistic experiments in contemporary American,
English, German, and French poetry (specially
"Dada"), which destructure semantics, lose most of
their impact within the context of the Portuguese
language. And of course: Brazilian literature is an
integral part of Western literature, but can only
function so automatically when it does not abandon
the specific problems posed by the language.
Much of one's effort was located in this arena;
unfortunately, these efforts were largely ignored.

§ From the beginning, long before one had a
clearer, phenomenological view of the problem,
the question of rhythm dominated. This demands
a more detailed explanation. The Czech language
formed the substratum of one's thought. In Czech,
the first syllable is invariably accentuated, which
means that hexameter feels appropriate to the

language and is therefore uninteresting, since it is redundant. This is why one found Czech classics written in hexameter virtually unreadable. In this regard, Czech is the opposite of French, which accentuates the last syllable, and for which the anapaest is appropriate and redundant. However, Portuguese and Brazilian literature do not rely on the "quality" but rather the "quantity" of syllables, which happens inauthentically – or rather, by ignoring the reality of what is being spoken – except, one must repeat emphatically, in Bossa Nova. Therefore, one's challenge was to turn the Portuguese language into hexametric. This was a challenge because, despite being innate to us, hexameter's rhythm is absolutely opposite to the Portuguese language's "spirit," and because hexameter creates, both directly and ironically, an epic and dramatic mood suitable for communicating one's message (which was always about groundless existence). However, it was equally clear that one's use of hexameter excluded writing poetry, as this would have been a form of inauthentic archaism and sheer affectation. Much later, Theo Spanudis' poetry provided hard proof of how hexameter defeats itself in poetry through an internal contradiction. Therefore, if one were challenged by the Portuguese language to write in hexameter, one had to write prose – preferably, essays. But the hexameter issue remained hidden in the text so that the reader would feel it but not be consciously aware of it. The reader would feel some strangeness in the text, but not be able to pinpoint it, and this could only be done if the hexameter was imperfect, which would also eliminate monotony. Sentences would end on an accentuated syllable, emphatically breaking up the epic flux of the discourse. The result was satisfactory, but disappointing: satisfactory in that several young people unconsciously copied one's style – proof that the rhythm did reach a noticeable level – but disappointing in that several critics assumed the text's strangeness resulted from one's imperfect grasp of the language rather than a self-imposed structure.

§ One must confess another problem with rhythm. Hexameter is a *Gestalt* made up of dactyls, although it is not the only form traditionally available. Pentameter and the combination of both hexameter and pentameter, the elegiac couplet, emanate an ever fascinating, magic hammering. A perfect rhythm would be to use hexameter to reach a climax and then pentameter to reach an anti-climax, according to Schiller's recipe: *"Im Hexameter steigt des Springquells silberne Säule, Im Pentameter drauf fällt sie melodisch herab."*[5]

5. "In the hex- ameter rises the fountain's silvery column, in the pentameter aye falling in melody back." Translation by S. T. Coleridge.

However, one soon discovered the rupture that characterises pentameter is intolerable as prose because it does not interrupt the flow of linear thought but rolls over it. Consequently, the elegiac couplet, despite remaining as two lines of poetry, loses the elegiac character of the prose. Later, when one learned about semantic rhythm in the Old Testament (for example: the mountains leapt like goats and the hills like sheep; or, you are like the

sweet rose and the lily of the valley), one grasped
the possibility of an almost pentametric rupture
through meaning. One imagined what it would
have been like if Homer had met the author of the
Song of Songs, and vice-versa. One tried to introduce
into one's texts semantic rhythm as a counterpoint
to syllabic rhythm, which progressively became
second nature. The danger of using semantic
rhythm lies, however, in the imagistic seduction
caused by metaphors. In other words: the sheep
and the lily of the valley become more important
than the hills and the beloved; the signifier more
important than the signified. The solution to this
problem emerged spontaneously and became one's
writing method: the text must be rhythmic not on
two, but three levels. On the syllabic level, imperfect
hexameter was the obvious choice for creating a
sonorous rhythm — except in violent diatribes (such
as answering offensive criticism in the newspapers),
when a flood of iambs seemed more appropriate.
On the word level, semantic rhythm must be used
sparingly, which is very difficult because images
tend to multiply spontaneously, and early on one
learned to mistrust "intuition" and spontaneity.
The defenders of "intuition" are likely not familiar
with it on a practical level. And on the level of
message, the rhythm must be geometric: structured
rhythmically like a flat figure that is imposed by the
message itself. If the message is dialectic, the figure
must be triangular; if the message is linear and
uninterrupted, it must be circular. This would be
one's "style": three rhythmic levels with a virtually

unlimited play of sympathies and antipathies between the levels. The Portuguese language thus became an instrument of engagement, to be used in an infinite game that changed during the course of play – which meant one changed with it. In other words: in a disciplined and enthusiastic way, one gradually became a Brazilian essayist.

§ The hybrid form of the essay, which lies between poetry and prose, philosophy and journalism, aphorism and speech, academic treatise and vulgarisation, criticism and the critiqued, is a universe in itself and an appropriate *habitat* for whoever is "exposed upon the mountains of the heart" (Rilke). Whoever practices this form, whoever lives essayistically (in other words, those for whom life itself is a preparation for essay writing), knows that the problem of the essay's subject is never clear. Or, to be precise: it is negatively clear. In the essay's universe everything is a subject and the problem lies in having to choose from such a rich array of subjects. However, to be honest, this statement is also incorrect. The choice of subject is imposed by the choice of rhythm. The essay's rhythm calls for its subject. Therefore, it is not so much a case of the medium being the message, but of the medium demanding its message. This is why this chapter seeks to communicate the motives behind one's choice of rhythm, but will not waste any time presenting the motives for one's choice of subject. To recapitulate: one's choice of rhythm was imposed by the dialectic between the

Portuguese language and the linguistic structure that shaped us; hence, the subjects of the resulting essays were imposed by their rhythms. However, despite their rhythms the subjects have been and shall always be variations on a single subject: the problem of engagement within a groundless situation. This is because one's own life (one's essay-life[6]) has been a variation on that subject, which could be aphoristically described as the " search for faith, in disgrace."

6. In Portuguese Flusser does a word play, vida-ensaio, but the word ensaio can be translated as both **essay** and **rehearsal**, or even **sketch**. So essay-life could also be read as life-rehearsal, or sketched-life. The idea of the essay as a rehearsal points to the very notion of groundlessness that Flusser explores. The idea of life as a constant sketch that is continuously changed and never pinned down or finished and varnished. Never fixed.

§ However, the essay's ambivalence lies in its character, which is both monologic and dialogic. In other words: the essay is a monologue that seeks a reply. For the essayist, culture is a linguistic fabric woven on a loom on which the writer plays with the threads. If the essayist wants a partner, he must engage with the loom and not the fabric. Dialogue is only possible on the level of the loom and not the fabric. This was the functional aspect of one's loneliness and isolation. During the early 1950s, one's problem was the following: how to penetrate the fabric of the Portuguese language in order to reach the loom on which it was woven? Theoretically, the answer was obvious: by reading as much as one could of the literature from every field, not so much to grasp its messages, but to encounter the authors at work. In any case, the messages were not interesting because one had already learned to doubt any "explanation" or "teaching." A practical solution for the problem emerged, however, in the *Literary Supplement* of *O Estado de São Paulo*. This

Vilém Flusser

was a periodical that existed, on its own, in a curious enclave within the local cultural context. The newspaper published news and commentaries within a global context, comparable to newspapers in other large urban centres and inspired by the cosmopolitan character of the decadent, pseudo-aristocracy from the State of São Paulo – as well as the 19th-century liberalism characteristic of this sector of the pseudo-aristocracy. Perhaps this is why, together with its reactionary ideology, the newspaper did not accurately depict the Brazilian situation – although it had a powerful influence on it. An examination of the *Estado*'s role during the period of liberal democracy and the period directly following it would undoubtedly provide a revealing account of the Brazilian cultural context.

§ However, its *Literary Supplement* had a certain autonomy within the newspaper. It was "apolitical" (meaning, it was "open to several trends, except the most extreme ones" – which obviously meant it was liberal in the 19th-century sense, as much as the newspaper that produced it), and less of a channel for literary critique. But it provided a somewhat unstructured arena for essayists from all over Brazil. The *Supplement* could be read in at least two ways: as a more or less random clearinghouse for information about the Brazilian cultural scene, and as a laboratory for developing the future culture of Brazil. In a radical sense, one followed the latter route: one read the *Supplement* not for what its contributors wrote but to see *how* they wrote and to contribute to it later. This had an immediate formal effect: the majority of essays published in the *Supplement* were two columns long – four typed pages. Hence, this determined the size of one's essays. This was a para-poetic limitation that forced us to struggle not only against and within the rules of the language, but also against and within the rules of the *Supplement*. This limitation proved fruitful (as every limitation is, given the dialectic between "limitation/freedom"). When one left the *Supplement* several years later, one's lack of limits, one's "freedom," became painfully obvious.

§ In sum: the moment one decided to engage with Brazilian culture, one became a potential contributor to the *Literary Supplement* of *O Estado de São Paulo*. The immediate problem was how to transform this potential into action. Or: how to break through the perfidy of human matter named the "*O Estado de São Paulo* newsroom." This took us directly to the core of engaging with Brazilian culture. The initial surprise was that, despite being an enclave of privilege within Brazilian culture, the *Supplement* was easy to enter – and therefore unfulfilling as a challenge. The second surprise was that, from the moment of acceptance, one was part of an enclave with which one barely agreed. The third surprise was that the published essays' effect (their feedback) was fast, relatively wide, and very superficial, hardly corresponding with the intensity of one's engagement. And the last (and most painful) surprise was the realisation that one's contribution to the *Supplement* did not confer any influence upon it: one's contribution was "irresponsible," or only an individual concern, which intensified one's sense of isolation. These surprises (which multiplied in every field) contributed to one's eventual disengagement – including from the *Supplement*. In short: the taste of defeat emerged in one's early and easy victories. This was the spirit in which one's engagement as a whole began.

§ In describing the dialogues of the 1950s and 60s – which are, in a way, on-going today (although one's gradual move to Europe has changed the channels) – one has to guard against the perfidy of memory. In the course of this book, the strongest resistance encountered has been a reluctance to acknowledge the social decadence (although secondary) caused by the Nazi catastrophe. One was born into a traditional elite against which one rebelled – but one was a part of it. During the 1940s there was social degradation, but also a reformulation of the social hierarchy: in Prague one saw the division of society organised by cultural levels; one occupied an exalted level within this hierarchy. In São Paulo, one was forced to accept a socio-economic hierarchy in which one occupied a relatively low level. This was not a conscious preoccupation at the time because social (and economic) vanity was not so developed in us and because there were more important ethical, epistemological, and ontological problems to worry about. In writing this book, however, the social degradation of that period reveals itself as a barrier imposed by memory, which proves it was repressed.

§ During this period, one's engagement with culture resulted in one's social reorientation, via criteria resembling those in Prague, and one's reinsertion into the corresponding level one occupied in Prague. Thanks to this engagement, one gradually began to occupy the social role reserved for one at birth. Although honesty begs the question of whether this return to one's original social position was a motive for engagement, the answer seems clear that: it was not. One never sought, at least on a conscious level, to become socially prominent. From this point onwards – at least as a method for writing this book – it is necessary to point out that one no longer represses problems relating to one's social position. However, a new type of resistance is emerging, demanding a new strategy: the fact that one tends to reduce the importance of one's role in Brazilian culture, either because of a new type of modesty or in order to reduce one's own responsibility. The danger this attitude poses is dialectic: by resisting, one falsifies testimony by understating it; by fighting resistance, one risks exaggerating the importance of the events reported here. The second danger is reinforced by a tendency towards self-praise and ego worship – a tendency one finds difficult to relinquish. The following testimony will seek to navigate between Scylla and Charybdis. One must state immediately that the following dialogues are important for both the present and future of Brazilian Culture.

DIALOGUE I

§ When looked at from the perspective of "information," there is a fundamental difference between dialogue and discourse that is not sufficiently accounted for by current research. Discourse is a process through which existing information is transmitted by emitters who hold information to receivers who "must" be informed. Discourse therefore seeks to propagate information in and through time. This makes discourse traditional and conservative, as well as dynamic and progressive: traditional, because the receiver remains connected to the information sources in his or her culture; conservative because discourse preserves the information available within a given culture; dynamic, because discourse carries information from the past to the future; progressive, because discourse ramifies the available information into channels that reach an increasing number of receivers, allowing this information to infiltrate ever wider layers of the culture. Given its character, discourse creates a specific existential climate for those who engage with it (e.g., advertising people, charismatic leaders, preachers, teachers, etc.). These people possess "valid" information, or "values," and they dedicate themselves to transmitting these "values" to others. However, this situation poses a problem for those who engage with discourse but begin to doubt the "validity" of the transmitted information. This problem will be discussed in this book in relation to one's engagement as a university teacher and "journalist."

§ Dialogue, on the contrary, is a process through which several information holders exchange dubious and partial information (or at least doubtful information) in order to reach a synthesis that could be considered "new information." Dialogue seeks the elaboration or "creation" of new information. This gives dialogue a revolutionary and circular, non-progressive character: revolutionary, because dialogue tries to leap from a contradictory level (doubted information) to a new, thetic level (that is, new information accepted by those who participate in the process); "circularly non-progressive," because structurally dialogue is a closed circuit (although the number of participants may theoretically increase within relatively narrow limits), and because the potential synthesis of information does not necessarily extend beyond the circle of participants. Given its character, dialogue creates a specific existential climate for those engaged with it (e.g., politicians – in the strictest sense of that term – and what are generally identified as philosophers, artists, and essayists). These are people who possess dubious and suspected information and dedicate themselves to submitting their information for testing so that it will become "valid" information – in other words, "values." The object of the following discussion and reminiscences will be the challenges posed by this climate.

Vilém Flusser

§ Additionally, another word should be said about methodology. Until now, this book has traced an approximately chronological line. However, this line is subject to doubt, on several levels. Chronology marks time as a flow, starting in the past and moving towards the future along a metric ruler etched with regular intervals (years, hours, and minutes). This is an approximately logarithmic ruler on which the initial minutes cover more space than the final years. However, chronology falsifies memory, since there are periods in the temporal flow that refuse to be measured, even logarithmically; or because they occupy segments on the ruler in which every minute counts; or because they occupy segments in which the flow of time is almost stagnant. The scale of memorised time is existential and hard to quantify (a methodological problem for a future de-historicised historiography). Nonetheless, this book attempted an approximate chronology for various reasons. One reason is that, until now, our life has been more about passivity and passion than activity and action – which means that life followed the general context of events, which was measured chronologically. The other reason is that the periods analysed, up until now, are sufficiently distant to be de-existentialised, to a certain point. One doubts whether the "We" of those periods is still the same "We" of today. This reified past may therefore be advantageously subjected to a chronology. From this point forward, however, the phenomenon will change radically. The life to be narrated will be more interesting as an assembly of actions than a collection of passions (even though the passionate aspect of these actions must not be obscured). Also, the motives that propel such a life are still present today. Chronology therefore no longer serves as an adequate descriptive method; other criteria must be sought.

Alex Bloch

§ The term "genius," although shabby and romanticised – and therefore to be avoided as much as possible – does impose itself in certain cases and must be humbly accepted when it does. This is one such case. However, here lies a problem. The genius manifests him- or herself in an opus by using a specific model to manipulate a particular reality, so that we are obliged to admit two things: that the model encompasses us and that reality has been manipulated in a wholly irreproachable way. This distinguishes the genius from the mere dreamer, as well as the meagre technician. The dreamer envisions a model that encompasses us, but cannot realise it. And the technician manipulates reality with irreproachable perfection, but uses a model one can overcome. In the case of Alex Bloch, the issue is this: his genius is manifested in the way he lives. His life is his opus. Reality, which he manipulates perfectly through a model that encompasses us, is his *being-in-the-world*. This creates a problem, because this kind of opus does not allow those who come into contact with it a humble and contemplative distance; it becomes a vortex, sucking the critic into its core. To have been (and still be) a part of Alex Bloch´s life is a privilege (and act of resolve) that permanently colours every experience and act.

§ Like us, Alex is a Prague Jew and a Brazilian immigrant who has accepted a groundless existence. But that is where the similarities end. With merciless honesty and truth (merciless with himself and the world at large), Bloch not only accepts the absurdity of every thought and action (especially any attempt "to explicate" and "engage with the world"), but also the vacuity of the "Self." "To live" for him means to grasp the *aistheton* of the moment, to be completely immersed in the concreteness of every instant. "The concrete" may be a natural or cultural environment, another person, or an idea. To live means to lose oneself in concreteness and become fused with it. This attitude cannot be reduced, however, to waiting passively for "adventure," because the flow of concreteness is slow and tends to stagnate in the daily grind. This situation generates apathy and tedium, which are synonymous with death. Life's horizons are apathy and tedium, not physical death. That is why the art of living is to travel from lived experience to lived experience, from adventure to adventure on every level of concreteness. Much later, one compared Bloch's practical attitude with the theories of Vicente Ferreira da Silva. The contrast between the two has served as a high point in one's life.

§ In order to generate concreteness it is necessary to wear several masks or "personalities." For example: to be a seller of technical books in São Paulo; a *guaraná* buyer in the Bahian countryside; assistant to a Buddhist monk in Suzano; an employee of a Jew in Bom Retiro and of a brothel in Liberdade; a tram conductor; a TV technician; an explorer in the Araguaia river; to live with monks in Goiás; to be a musicologist specialised in African chants; to practice symbolic logic and yoga; to study electronic music and building with concrete; to speculate on the stock exchange and in real estate; to be a worker in Stockholm; to live with a Brazilian painter and an esoteric group in London; to practice Catholicism and group dynamics. The obvious problem, that of wearing so many masks one betrays one's Self, does not apply in Bloch's case. For him, the "Self" is an empty hook upon which any mask may be hung. Bloch authentically becomes whichever mask he wears. What differentiates him from the "real" musicologist or the Bahian wise guy is "simply" his awareness, that he choses to be this or that and then chooses no longer to be it.

§ So this is the art of living, in the real sense of the term. The only working categories are aesthetic: intensity, variety, and emotional or informative charge. The high aesthetic intensity that characterises Bloch, the almost physical pain he feels when faced with kitsch, posturing, and pompous grandiloquence, are the only values he lives by. "To become fused with concreteness" is precisely this: to separate the concrete from the aesthetically repulsive ideological scum that covers it; to live in the raw and bare beauty of what is concrete – and which is beautiful precisely for being raw and bare. Bloch's life may be defined, therefore, as engagement against what is false, and in favour of what is absurdly true.

§ There are, of course, models for this type of existence: Hesse's *Steppenwolf*, Kafka's *K.*, Camus' *L'Etranger*, and perhaps even Goethe's *Mephistopheles*. However, these models appear as abstractions when compared to the concreteness of Bloch's lived experience. Bloch was only moved by a model once: Beckett's *Molloy*. However, one could ask whether this was due to self-recognition or a momentary submersion into concreteness, as in all of his lived experiences. In the end, no model (abstraction) characterises him. For him, theories are another type of reality and not explanations or functional models for an "object-reality." Freud must be experienced in the way one experiences the Oedipus complex and not as a discourse in which the Oedipus complex functions as a subject.

§ Because of Bloch's radically concrete mode of living, dialogue with him cannot be dialogue in the Socratic sense. Our dialogue has never been two monologues seeking synthesis. The exchanges between us have always been curiously uneven. Effectively, our dialogue has taken two forms: the first, in which there was a subject to be dialogued, and the second, in which one's Self was the subject. The first followed a classic course: one had read a book, seen a painting, watched a film, or conceived an idea. When Bloch arrived, one rushed to tell him about the experience, for two opposite reasons: first, to share the new information and act as a perception organ for him, aimed at the world (one was aware and gladly accepted that Bloch used us as a perception instrument); second, to see how Bloch would dissect the information, reducing it to its most refined elements. Bloch was also aware that one used him as an instrument for refining one's own ideas, a role he gladly accepted. During one's report, Bloch immediately called one's attention to the internal inconsistencies of what was being reported and the external inconsistencies between oneself and the report. In most cases, his critique was enough to reduce the book, film, or idea to vacuous grandiloquence. In these cases, one shared with Bloch the hilarious experience of unmasking — a hilarity that was not cynical because it afforded the pure and liberating experience of freeing oneself from mystifying ideologies. In a few cases, however, the report resisted Bloch's critique: the book, music, film, or idea held its ground. This was the case with Wittgenstein, Klee, Handel's *Messiah*, Stockhausen's first compositions, Bergman, and one's own grand idea that it was necessary to existentialise Neopositivism. In these cases, Bloch would take one's position, delve deep into the subject, and seek with second-degree introspection. The result was that one gradually discovered in unison why these phenomena were "valid" for us. The result was also a liberating exhilaration, but of a different type. The first exhilaration provided the lived experience to be "archived"; the second allowed one to continue conscious study (but not Bloch, obviously). This type of dialogue always ended in uproarious laughter and a revelatory liberation.

§ The second form of dialogue between us, in which one's Self was the subject, followed another characteristic course: one had written an essay or was writing a book and one sat there waiting impatiently for Bloch to arrive, in order to read to him what had been written. Bloch listened with concentrated attention (one never had a more attentive audience), critiquing only the aesthetic and stylistic slips during the reading. No insincerity in the text escaped him. In fact, Bloch was living proof that intellectual dishonesty is articulated aesthetically. For this reason, one always accepted his critiques. Because, as merciless as they were, and despite hurting one's pride, they were simply always true. Bloch had the gift of delving to the core of honesty. One's writing style and one's way of thinking are mostly the result of these on-going and disciplined purifications. After the reading and initial critique, Bloch would move on to an analysis of the existential climate, inserting the text into one's own context and making clear where one had failed to reach one's proposed aim. The dual result was that one felt destroyed while Bloch was amused. One's resolve was always to do better in the future. Nevertheless, one published what had been written because one needed to communicate, and because nobody except Bloch would identify the fundamental flaws in the text. This is what characterises the essay form: each attempt is essentially imperfect, but serves as a bridge for the writer to reach perfection in the next one. For Bloch, though, one's published work was uninteresting: he could not comprehend the need to communicate or the vanity of self-affirmation. The act of writing was interesting to him only as a method of self-discovery – an act from which he was exempt, since one wrote on his behalf. This second type of dialogue was challenging, but for Bloch it was amusing.

§ This was an emotionally charged relationship: it signified friendship. However, for Bloch, who eschewed any type of emotional involvement (because it curtailed the freedom to seek a variety of experience), the relationship was casual, although very interesting. When Bloch felt in danger of becoming emotionally enmeshed, he brutally severed the connection, renewing it much later in a milder form. One respected his decision because one sensed that, from his perspective, it was an honest decision. He distanced himself for "mental hygiene" (Bloch's words), which had to be respected. Despite the aloofness, he continued to be one's critic *par excellence*, which in a certain way, one kept on reserve. One had to hold one's ground in relation to Bloch, which means he is an *alter ego*.

Vilém Flusser

§ If the relationship with Bloch is structured as
two parallel lines initiating at the same point, then
separating and crossing on multiple levels and
finally parting again, the relationship with Vargas
is structured like this: two lines that converge
from opposite poles. (Naturally, this analysis is
provisional: both processes are on-going and extend
into an unknown future.) However, the personalities
of Bloch and Vargas, which are different in every
other respect, intersect in two places: radical
honesty and incredible diversity. The essential,
existential difference between the two is this: Bloch
tends towards pure passivity and Vargas towards
intense activity in multiple fields of engagement.
As an engineer (builder of Brazil's most important
dams and roads), theoretician of soil mechanics
(with international standing), central to Brazilian
industrial development, university professor (with
a significant influence on academic life), essayist on
philosophy and science, literary critic (especially
on Romantic and pseudo-Romantic English
poetry), editor, original thinker in the fields of
religion and politics, and with a vision that is both
universal and centred, Vargas is an anachronism in
an age of specialisation and departmentalisation:
an integral and universal man in the Renaissance
sense of the term. But there are two problems
around his person: one with internal origins and
the other with external ones. The first relates to
his extreme modesty and consequent difficulty in

doing justice to his rich personality. The second relates to an increasing disparity between his *being-in-the-world* and the stream of current events. The result is a curious dialectic: the more he engages with the world, the more he alters it; the more he does not recognise himself in the world, the more he is rejected by it. His is an exceptional case of sustained and disciplined praxis based on lucid and sophisticated theory, which nonetheless does not result in an authentic alteration of the Self. This is why Vargas' life is tragic in the Greek sense of the term: a hero who the *Erinyes* pursue – *Erinyes* who he provoked and continues to provoke. The dramatic energy Vargas radiates is the basis for our uniting, dialogical friendship.

§ Superficially, Vargas is one's mentor *in rebus brasiliensibus* in the sense that he introduced us to the multiple facets of Brazilian reality. If one felt sheltered by Brazilian reality for decades, and sought to modify it by modifying oneself, Vargas' intermediation and mediation made this happen. However, once one decided, painfully, to distance oneself from such an enterprise, it was also due to the rupture one felt between Vargas and the world. This rupture proved to be the great theme of one's dialogue with Vargas – and continues to this day. Summing up: for years one sought with increasing despair to tear the cloak that Vargas wore, protecting himself against the flow of things that were his enemies. One did this not only to save him but also to save oneself, since one felt increasingly connected to him. This struggle, which could be called "agony," and in which one always played the role of aggressor (even though he usually instigated the aggression), became the atmosphere in which one acted. Everything one wrote, and continues to write is destined to be critiqued by Bloch – and to unravel Vargas. If Vargas resisted, one was defeated. But if Vargas surrendered, was not this one's own defeat?

§ In order to solve the problem, one must return to the 1930s and one's formative years. Those years revealed to one the fragility of reason, and this was cause for despair: reason ennobled humanity and its fragility allowed the eruption of irrationality among the masses. From Vargas' perspective, that period also revealed the fragility of reason, but this was cause to rejoice: reason was what dehumanised and mechanised humanity and the fragility of reason allowed the eruption of powers that were previously repressed – truly productive powers. Like Vargas, one was affected by the crisis of reason, but both of us experienced a divided loyalty. One felt the alluring beauty of the irrational eruption, despite fearing its mortal danger. For example: Dada, Surrealism, and the English Neo-Romantics. Vargas felt the alluring beauty of reason despite mistrusting it. For example: contemporary physics, different types of mathematics, new methods in *technics* and administration, and the formal rigour of rational arguments. The absurdity of divided loyalty was that one opted for reason's danger, although one's temperament skewed towards the irrational side of things. And Vargas opted for those "new powers" (in the archaic sense), even though his temperament skewed towards the technical and scientific. One was a frustrated rationalist (due to one's temperament and the course of things) and Vargas was a frustrated irrationalist (due to his temperament and the course of things after the war). One thing, however, seems unquestionable: one is not surprised by current events. The rupture of reason means placing reason in the service of irrationality, and therefore in the service of mass culture. Current events are nothing but the obvious consequences of Stalinism, Nazism, and the *New Deal* of the 1930s. There is no rupture. For Vargas, current events are terribly disappointing because the leading tendencies of the 1930s were repressed. It seems therefore as if one had diagnosed these tendencies "better" than Vargas: as the eruption of the masses and not something new.

§ This means a profound difference in our diagnosis and prognosis of internal and external situations, although it also means we are complementary – which is useful for exposing reality. Starting from the diagnostic side, one's interest always centred upon the defeat of reason: Wittgenstein, Kafka, Husserl, Surrealism, and the failure of the Russian Revolution. Vargas' interest always centred on the eruption of irrationality: Jun Lawrence, the art of fantasy, and Nazism. There were points of convergence, however, for instance when irrationality became reasoned and when reason became irrational: Heidegger, Ortega y Gasset, and Rilke. The complementary nature of our temperaments was revealed in these points of convergence and it formed the basis for our dialogues, which sought to diagnose the situation and one's position within it. Three topics were preferred: Nazism, aesthetics, and the Brazilian situation. To sum up the discussion: one diagnosed Nazism as a movement that alienated the masses, a precursor to the mass alienation of today. Vargas diagnosed Nazism as an articulation of deeply repressed tendencies that manifested themselves as "evil" for having been repressed and which, if acknowledged, could be highly productive. (In this case, one held to a Marxist model and Vargas to a Jungian model.) One always saw artistic articulation as the human spirit imposing order on rebellious and perfidious matter and the "beauty of art" as the human spirit's victory over the world's resistance. Vargas saw artistic articulation as the revelation of an essence hidden in the relationship between humanity and the world. For him the "beauty of art" was "the greatness of truth." One conceived of the Brazilian situation as a great agglomeration of people (miserable and exploited by a domestic caste system, as well as external interests); a situation in which one saw new tendencies (both from within and without) that pointed towards a cultural synthesis that could establish one of the models for a "new Man" (as in China, for instance). One always began these analyses from one's linguistic experience and one's engagement was aimed at this objective. Vargas conceived of the Brazilian situation as a country on the path of slow and profound revolution, situated within a South American context, and which would eventually adopt a decisive role on the international stage – but potentially lose its identity in the process. These were three purportedly disconnected themes in which one saw reality in incongruent ways. Ultimately, however, there was and is a common substratum – a convergence of categories: in all three topics of our dialogue, the rational is opposed to the irrational, and one always sought the absorption of the irrational by reason, whereas Vargas typically sought the "acceptance" of the irrational. In the case of Nazism, one opted against it because there was no possibility of assimilating such barbarity. Vargas opted for – let us say, a "sublimation" of Nazism. In the case of art, one opted for innovative experiences that sought to formalise lived experience. Vargas opted essentially against any attempt to formalise lived experiences. In the case of the Brazilian reality, one opted for a conscious rationalisation of irrational tendencies on a new plane, while Vargas opted for a limited rationalisation that permitted the eruption of a Brazilian temperament (largely irrational) onto the larger human stage.

§ Our dialogues modified both of us. One was forced to admit the pertinence of Vargas' analyses on several occasions. Effectively: Nazism was not

only a mass movement, it was a depreciation of
repressed tendencies which, if seen in isolation, were
very exciting when articulated – for example, by
Nietzsche. One had not seen this because, at close
range, Nietzsche was nothing more than another of
the many deceitful Nazi slogans, and because Nazi
reality was anti-Nietzschean. Vargas taught us to
see with a more detached perspective. Effectively:
in art, there is an element that "reveals its essence";
an element that cannot be exhausted by formal
analyses and which escapes an immediate critique.
Vargas taught us to accept this mystery in art, which
one had always felt but had not had the courage to
admit (due to one's anti-Romantic engagement).
Curiously, one felt this mystery more intimately
than Vargas because one's artistic sensibility was
more developed than his. Effectively: one saw that
it was worth engaging with Brazil, if only because
there is an indescribable feature of the Brazilian
character that deserves preservation and a stronger
influence on the larger human scene. Vargas not
only taught us to see this, but also demonstrated
it quintessentially through his *being-in-the-world*.
How Vargas modified us may be summarised in
this way: one came to admit, although with serious
reservations, that there were values (all of them
extra-rational) worth living for (and possibly even
dying for) after all. Vargas was therefore the motor
propelling one's engagement.

§ The alterations one produced in Vargas are
harder to identify. A double contradiction in

his personality provided the opening through which one could penetrate. The first was a contradiction between his human decency, with his visceral humanism, and his global, de-existentialising, theoretical anti-humanism. The second contradiction was between his technological engagement, in favour of Europeanising the environment, and his Romantic yearning for bygone days. (This contradiction was not present in Vicente Ferreira da Silva, who greatly influenced Vargas; consequently, the dialogue with Vicente occurred in an entirely different environment.) At any rate, one thing seems certain: the dialogues shook Vargas to his foundation, but he resisted. This will be discussed shortly.

§ From one's own standpoint, differences grew rather than shrank over the course of our dialogue. Although Vargas' influence had contributed powerfully to our engagement, it also contributed to a growing pessimism. The world Vargas represented and engaged in seemed ever more intolerable and anachronistic, and the way he eschewed *the new* proved this existentially. The vision one had of Brazil revealed itself to be more illusory, and the vision one had of the "new Man" (linked so intimately to one's own Brazilian engagement) revealed itself to be a projection designed to obscure the absurdity of the current situation. One felt obliged to measure certain values against reality and admit their vacuity – precisely because Vargas pointed out this possibility. Subsequently, despite being greatly enriched by Vargas, one was back at the beginning: recognizing the absurdity of any form of engagement. Vargas, on the other hand, opted in favour of more engagement in several fields, which he knew to be in vain — a knowledge of which one contributed. His pessimism (equally radical to one's own) therefore continued to be concealed by his actions. And paradoxically, action for Vargas was the opium that allowed him not to see the world and himself in it.

§ The testament of this intense dialogue seems melancholic, relative to its results. The profound reality we both experienced contradicts this, though. What our dialogues questioned was not this problem or that (these were merely pretexts), but what might be called "human vocation." This is why our dialogue occurred (even at frivolous moments) in a religious environment. This environment revealed our complementary nature to be extremely fertile. One learned not only to tolerate the other's vocation, but also to recognise one's other self in it. On this level, our dialogue was not about coming to understand the other's position, but recognising it and recognising oneself in it. Vargas was our opposite in his way of thinking and acting in the world. And this was the missing element in us. Through one's contact with Vargas, one became whole. One saw the world inside out — and oneself inside out. The same thing happened to Vargas, who immersed one in obscure regions where one did not have the courage to venture, even during the moments of greatest despair, since Vargas revealed only the most seductive features of such depths. In turn, one humanised Vargas and taught him painfully to see beauty in the existential dimensions of the grand ideas he upheld. This was an important aspect of our dialogue: one existentialised Vargas' essences (his "great inhuman and anti-human concepts"), and Vargas teased out what was essential in one's existential decisions. Nevertheless, there existed some asymmetry: one was able to absorb Vargas' "essences" and adapt one's decisions accordingly. Given the rigidity of every "essential" thought and action (of "faith" or "fanaticism"), however, Vargas was never able to absorb the existential impact that one represented. He was always on the defensive, afraid of crumbling — something one did not fear, having already experienced it.

§ The most radical aspect of our dialogue was this: one's very existence problematised the other's. We were mutually negating. This is the true religious dialectic (that which the Talmud and the Gospel call "love for the other"). One could not exist because of the other; therefore, one could not exist without the other. This dialectic can only be resolved in the Total Other. The clash of two existences, irreconcilable and therefore needing each other, created a Totality. In the beginning, neither of us recognised that our dialogue was "essentially" a prayer and a plea *de profundis*. This became more evident over time. Faced with provocation (and ambivalence), both of us were overwhelmed at times by humility, feeling almost viscerally that we were nothing but pawns of some unnameable Thing. But here we precipitously approach the Wittgensteinian border, so it is best to be quiet. After all, neither of our "agonies" is finished yet, and despite being opposites, we both feel encouraged by the enthusiasm to fulfil our diverging vocations.

Vicente Ferreira da Silva

§ Some existential situations resist theoretical analysis – despite the fact everyone frequently experiences them. Among these, the most characteristic is a person's death. To theorise this event means to generalise, and the death of another person cannot be generalised, because contrary to a thing, a person cannot be easily defined by categories. Every attempt to label or classify the other – for example, within the categories of "friend," "relative," or "partner" – reifies the other. Their essence is lost: the other is irreplaceable. Any generalisation of the other's death through categorisation – such as the death of friends, relatives etc. – not only falsifies the phenomenon, but is existentially revolting. One's father does not die, but something irreplaceable has disappeared from the world when he dies. One's friend did not die; Vicente died. Friendship is effectively born when one label is removed and another entirely unclassifiable one emerges from underneath it.

When the labels "philosopher," "bourgeois," "Brazilian," "Dora's husband," and a number of others are removed, and even the label "Vicente" is removed, what remains is a pulsating *sui generis* presence; one that is no longer present. This is what another's death teaches us: what Judeo-Christianity proposes, that every type of generalisation is a falsification of the phenomenon "other." This is the meaning of "soul." This is also why the basis of Vicente's own thought is false, sinful, and radically disputable. Vicente theorises the existential and generalises the concrete, therefore putting forth a worldview that is entirely false. He speaks of "the war," and yet has no understanding of any given war. He speaks of "Marxism," but has no comprehension of a given Marxist. He speaks of "Judaism," but has no particular Jew in mind. He speaks of "the sacred," but has no experience of sanctity. He does have incisive knowledge – thanks to such generalisations, but no comprehension – which (why not say it?) is tantamount to evil. A theoretical and de-existentialised type of evil, and not evil in his decisions and actions – but evil all the same. One is attracted to Vicente because this type of Evil is seductive. Hiding under his mask of theoretical beauty is its correlate: the temptation to save him by showing him his fundamental flaw. This was the nature of our dialogue.

§ Comparing Vicente to Bloch on the one hand and Vargas on the other is a useful method for examining the phenomenon of Evil. Like Bloch,

Vicente only recognised real life as lived experience: concreteness and immanence. That is how Bloch has lived, but Vicente theorised and glorified adventure. As a result, Bloch saw Vicente as the embodiment of a lie and Vicente saw Bloch as an unbearable, gut-wrenching trial. Like Vargas, Vicente preached a type of antihumanist irrationalism. With Vargas, however, the preaching unravels and becomes a concrete, living contradiction, thanks to his fundamental virtuousness and human decency. With Vicente, the preaching stuck and remained consistent because it never translated into concrete praxis. This resulted in a curious and wicked inversion: Vargas saw Vicente as a mentor, which Vicente accepted, since Vicente's thought was more consistent and radical than Vargas' – and yet, in reality, with its contradictions and open praxis, Vargas' thought surpassed Vicente's. Vargas' character engulfed Vicente. Vicente is nothing but a facet of Vargas, and Vargas' complexity seeks (desperately) to assimilate Vicente. Vicente is undoubtedly the greatest – possibly the only – Brazilian philosopher, if by "philosopher" one means a consistent and profound thinker. However, Vargas is much more than that. One could say that Vicente is an evil version of both Bloch and Vargas, since he lacks the breadth that is their saving grace. And that is the essence of evil: the lack of something. Inversely, goodness means plenitude, although, one has little concrete experience with goodness. Holiness is rare.

§ Despite the inherent evil that resided deep in the core of his thinking, Vicente was a captivating and fascinating presence, and a joyful one. This is because, when evil is theoretical, the Kantian abyss that separates it from the practical dimension does not allow it to be experienced as evil, either by the sender or the receiver of such messages. One can only imagine what would have happened if Vicente had magically become sovereign over the world and turned his theories into practice: genocide, social and economic anarchy, exploitation of the weak by the powerful, and fanatical persecution of the opposition. However, until we met Vicente, no one, not even Vicente himself, had tried to imagine this. The atmosphere surrounding Vicente was so de-existentialised that no one, neither supporters nor opponents, ever reached a concrete conclusion. Everyone at these amiable and joyful gatherings was free to talk about bloodbaths and Dantean destruction. Curiously, however, this could not be called "alienation" in the strictest sense of the term. Vicente's intention was not to conceal reality with bloody, fanatical projections. On the contrary, he wanted to extract concrete experiences from reality in order to penetrate its essential structure, which, for him, was an anti-Husserlian *mathesis*: general theoretical entities he called "gods." His was a radical research into essences — a radical ontology — and his method was a brand of anti-empiricism that was both anti-rational and anti-existentialising. This abstracting furore was incredibly original because it was in fundamental disagreement with both the traditional Platonism dominant in Brazil, and with phenomenology (although heavily nourished by it). The Brazilian critics, in their positivist eagerness to bestow European labels on everything, called it "Existentialism." And there could not be a more grotesque misunderstanding. The tendency to label everything, an encyclopaedist trait common among many Brazilian intellectuals, was not only shared by Vicente, but also taken to a level of paroxysm.

§ One's initial encounter with this universe produced an intense and vivifying shock, on several levels. One's intellect and experience had created a dialectical method for thinking and speculating that oscillated in this way: one was always attracted to theories and delighted in their beauty, but shortly sought to experience their concrete significance. This toing and froing between theory and praxis was the climate in which one continuously threw oneself against the railings of formal and transcendent structures, on the one hand, and the unformalisable and immediate immanence of otherness, on the other hand – which is precisely what spawned the vertigo of the abyss. Hence, one's encounter with Vicente's universe propelled us towards an incomparably fascinating mode of theory because it was a theory of experience (a self-negating one), and because one's attempt to experience it resulted in the experience of Evil. How was this possible? Had one not overcome the Good and Evil dialectic long ago? Had one not abandoned all valuation? Did one not float dangerously past Good and Evil, in a Nietzschean sense? How could Evil shock us? Who was this bourgeois within us that Vicente had frightened? Later, one gradually and painfully discovered that this bourgeois was the kernel of a Judaeo-Christian hidden in a dark corner inside us, which Vicente caused to re-emerge from the ashes. One saw Vicente as the living and devastating proof of the Lord's tortuous path: He revealed Himself through His own contradiction because, in Vicente, it was possible to love the sinner and hate the sin. One began to hate Vicente's thought but to love him; to love Vicente as one loves oneself, or despite his thinking and not because of it.

§ This is not the place to examine Vicente's thought, though. One has already dedicated several essays to the subject, both in the midst of the trauma following his death and afterwards. To analyse Vicente, to fully unpack his thought and its consequences, would be to grasp the absurd – a future task that will contribute significantly to the understanding of Brazilian culture and its development. Vicente represents a fundamental Brazilian "lift-off," a mid-twentieth century phenomenon of universal importance that was truncated by his death. A number of radical ideas that have disrupted contemporary Western philosophy, and which are generally associated with the "New Left," the hippie movement, the second "American Revolution," and the "Chinese Cultural Revolution," are not only prefigured by but well developed in Vicente's thought. Many of Vicente's ideas are still only hinted at in current global trends. What matters here, however, is not the analysis of his thought, but its dialogic function in our own encounters with him. The following reflections will take up this task.

§ Contrary to us, Vicente glorified adventure and war, but never experienced either one. He was a man of letters, who led a Guttenbergian, one-dimensional existence, submerged in the linear code of letters. But oh, what one-dimensionality! He was a voracious and insatiable reader who had absorbed information not only from the immense and colossal field of "culture," but also reorganised what he had read into a highly original, personalised system. This feat was possible due to two factors: his geographic and existential distance from many events, and his philosophical and religious zeal. His dreamy and penetrating gaze, as he presented the visions unfolding before him, is unforgettable. One felt as though one were watching a vital, historical film about human thought; a film with a single viewpoint illuminated by a passion for theory. His writing style served as a counterpoint: dense and academic, constantly on the brink of precious terminology, torn in unexpected places by flashes of violent poetry. Aesthetically speaking, Vicente's thought consisted of heavy clouds convulsing and discharging tension through lightning bolts and frightening thunder, but never culminating in vivifying rain. *"Welch Schauspiel! aber ach! ein Schauspiel nur!"* (Oh, what a show! But still! Only a show!) Faust would have said.

§ Witnessing such a spectacle, one could not remain passive. After all, one had not only read several of the authors Vicente referenced (especially the German Idealists and Nietzsche), but read them "closely" (in other words, within their own traditions) and considered the concrete significance of each. Heidegger will serve as an illustration of the skirmishes that ensued. In one's own mind, Heidegger (who had been a personal focus of interest directly before meeting Vicente) was someone who, above all else, extended and reformulated phenomenology. Heidegger's masterful analysis of *Sorge* (pre-occupation); his brilliant distinction between the future (the thing), the present (the Other), and the past (the instrument); and his dialectic between decadence and project – in other words, the step back from Being and its consequent unfolding into an existential time on the one hand, and into a *being-here* and *being-there* on the other – was for us an ontological and existential revelation, and an immediate challenge. Paradoxically, in a Heideggerian sense, one always felt in Heidegger that "*da stimmt etwas nicht*" (something is not right). But, at the time, one could not pinpoint what it was. Later, one came to discover that Heidegger's "weakness" lies in his use of language and his concept of the word as "the dwelling of Being." The terrible consequence of this is that Heidegger's ontology is not, properly speaking, an analysis of Being but of the verb "to be," since he loses Husserl's imperative *"die Dinge zu Wort kommen lassen"* (to let things speak for themselves). However, for Vicente, Heidegger had a completely different message. For him, Heidegger chased German Romantic thinking in the opposite direction, to its origin and beyond. He saw this as a type of Heideggerian *Nachdenken* (rethinking in a contrary sense) that was not speculation, but a sort of detective work, searching for the criminal (Being) and crime (*Seiendes*), hidden behind Idealism. In Vicente's mind, this *Nachdenken* (which Heidegger directed against Nietzsche, Hölderlin, Hegel, and Fichte, as well as the ontological premises of Idealism as a whole and "transcendentalism" in all its facets) was not only a philosophical method, but a religious one, as well. Pursuing, with the help of Heidegger, German Idealist thought (and by extension, Western thought *tout court*) to its origin and beyond, Vicente revealed the founding motives of Being (the gods) and Western thought's concealing action upon Being (its subject-form deformation). This pursuit, which Heidegger started, served as a therapy aimed at healing the Western malady (the profanation of Being through its humanisation on the one hand, and its objectification on the other). In this reading, Heidegger was revolutionary for undermining all the concealed origins of Western culture. Although both readings (ours and Vicente's) were not strictly speaking irreconcilable (both were based on rigorous readings of the texts), they resulted in two opposing views: an existentialised Heidegger and Vicente's simultaneously ontologised and politicised one. For the resulting dialogue, it did not matter whose view of Heidegger was most "correct." It did not matter, even from a formal perspective, because one saw *Being and Time* as the decisive text, whereas Vicente saw *Letter on Humanism* as the decisive text. What mattered is that one saw Heidegger's step-back as a step towards absurdity and nothingness; for Vicente it was a step closer to the sacred. What signified the Plenitude of Being for Vicente, one saw as nothingness (therefore sin and Hell), and what signified Being-as-such in its absurdity for us, Vicente saw as the sacred. For Vicente, to challenge what is given meant to go in search of life (orgy and feast), while for us, challenging what is given was tantamount to *hubris*, a form of beautiful but sinful heroism, such that it was imperative not to *challenge* what is given, but to go *with* what is given, so as to modify it. In sum: one sought to accept Being-as-such in order to act upon it (including one's own Being-as-such), while Vicente sought to remove Being-as-such (including his own "Self") in order to approach Trans-human immanence. The structure and the dynamic of his thought were therefore purely reactionary; under the mantle of this revolutionary attitude hid submission and passivity (which Vicente viewed as religious categories). His *hubris* was humbled before trans-human immanence — or, in other words, a pseudo-Greek paganism: pagan because it denied transcendence and pseudo-Greek because it was speculatively "superstitious." Vicente himself accepted this, despite resisting the prefix "pseudo" that one constantly threw at him. Towards the end of his life he almost tearfully accepted this "pseudo": a type of salvation, which he may have achieved in death.

§ Vicente's thoughts were altered by our dialogues – alterations caused by one's insistence in translating grand concepts and generalisations into concreteness and praxis – but the dialogues also opened up great horizons for oneself. An example: Vicente's worldview was an original synthesis of disparate readings. However, these readings were within a field obscured by the suspicious shadow of Nazism. One's own reading of the same texts had therefore been painful and demanded self-discipline. Vicente's fundamental idea about the founding structures of reality, the "establishing powers," was a synthesis of Otto's "Holiness," Eliade's mythological analyses, Jung's concept of "archetype," and – obviously – Heidegger's ontological analyses. What unified these disparate concepts (which Vicente made explicit) was the discovery that thought, sensibility, valuation, and consequently human action followed particular patterns that existed before humans. Therefore, individuals and societies did not act according to their own projects but within projects they participated in from birth. Biography and history did not emerge as stages upon which humans acted but as stages upon which humans made gestures prefigured by the powers that threw them on the stage – a puppet theatre in which "myths," "archetypes," or other trans-human powers pulled the strings. Although this vision of predetermined human activity and the illusory nature of human freedom did not surprise us (the only surprise was the poetico-Romantic terminology wrapped around the ancient, fatalist ideology of authors referenced by Vicente), and although this ideology seemed to have been demystified definitively by Hegel and Marx's analysis of the dialectic of freedom, there was still an aspect of it that was radically new at the time. This was effectively a version of immanentist and pragmatic fatalism (i.e., pre-determination comes from the individual, from his or her biological, psychological, and cultural situation, not from transcendent factors), and simultaneously a type of fatalism that allowed the individual to challenge the powers of pre-determination. If the trans-human powers that pre-determine us lie within, they made be discovered through introspection, and although one may not escape them, one may identify with them. One does not become free by this method. However, one finds freedom in discovering that one is merely an epiphenomenon of such powers, that one exists in freedom. This was a vision that coincided in several ways with "the discovery of a vocation, authenticity, and truth itself" that had preoccupied so much of one's existential analyses, even though one had performed the operation inside out. Inside out because finding one's vocation does not mean answering a call from without in order to overcome oneself, but discovering a calling within, in order to let go of the desire to overcome oneself. This means a vocation to exist as one is at the root and not a vocation to be what one "should" become. When one came to this realisation and discovered that Vicente's gods were all *di inferiores* – that they were trans-human because they were all subhuman – a new light shone upon one's viewpoint. All the establishing powers Vicente discussed, all these great entities that projected one's actions (i.e., "race," culture, social, and economic situation, to demystify his terminology) had been perfectly diagnosed by Vicente. They do indeed pull the strings by which one is suspended. However, they only represent one's infernal, inferior, subhuman side. In Rilke's words, they are calling forth "the shameless River God of the blood and his fearsome trident."[7] To live exclusively under their power would mean a hellish life (which was actually what Vicente recommended). There are other strings pulled by other powers, however, such as human decency, solidarity, love for another, love for ideas and ideals – other higher powers that are equally predetermining. Vicente sought in his own terms to expose the telluric side of the pantheon, but the uranic side escaped him, because it is not immanent to the human condition, but transcendent. Nevertheless, this uranic side is within us too (inside one's chest, as Kant says of the categorical imperative) and not up in some "heaven"

7. Flusser is paraphrasing R. M. Rilke's **The Duino Elegies**, 1912-22.

introduced by an "establishing power" as Vicente thought. One must seek to admit both sides of the pantheon because one's freedom lies precisely in this dialectic. One's freedom and responsibility lie in the dialectic between that which exists as it should (so profoundly analysed by Vicente) and that which should exist as it is but does not (which Vicente ignored, since he believed that what should exist is already included in the project of what is). And R. Otto's work on the idea of the Holy (especially his analysis of ritual enactment) demonstrates this very clearly: Judeo-Christianity is anti-magic because it reveals the other side of the pantheon, not because it suppresses Hell. Ritual enactment gives way to responsible action, not for denying the scene, but for adding a new dimension. Thus, Vicente's paganism (which was pseudo-pagan, because it was reactionary) opened for us a new view of Judeo-Christianity. Thanks to Vicente (albeit against his will), one re-established contact with transcendent religiosity in the following manner: Vicente was absolutely correct to say that one cannot be free if one does not attempt to accept all the powers hidden within us and which predetermine one's life. If one did not do this, one would be living a lie. However, this alone is not enough, and by itself would mean descending into barbarity and evil. The succeeding step should be accepting all the internal potentialities that one has not yet become, but which one must become to be free. These powers will act upon what one is and how one asserts oneself. These powers alter us – or, better still: one will alter oneself, thanks to such powers. Having theoretically shown us Hell, Vicente opened a path to one's search for Heaven (a frustrated but vitally important search). Having shown us paganism, in such a fascinating manner, Vicente opened Judeo-Christianity. Vicente thus marked one's entire life.

§ Vicente's death was a terrible experience that truncated our dialogue at the exact moment when, after an intense struggle, both participants were prepared to follow a path that neither had initially considered possible: the path of Judeo-Christianity. This hard task fell upon one's shoulders, after being abandoned by one's *frenemy*. Others could not participate in this project — not even Vargas — because, what proof did one have to show that Vicente was on the threshold of changing paths? Would not such a statement betray the work of one's dead friend and, still worse, betray a shared secret? But in the end, what did all of it mean? Two competitors, one in theory an orgiastic neo-pagan who ironically contemplated praxis, the other an uprooted individual with no faith in any sort of reality, who had just emerged from an encounter with oriental meditation, mutually converting each other to Judeo-Christianity? No one would have believed such a thing — still worse, one began to doubt it oneself. At a crucial moment, a few days before his death, Vicente was preparing himself to start fresh with everything; one was getting ready to write *The History of the Devil*.[8] What remained later is this second part of our truncated dialogue,

8. Flusser, V. **The History of the Devil**. Univocal Publishing, Minneapolis 2014, Trans. By Rodrigo Maltez Novaes.

suspended in mid-air, since the dead do not answer, except inside us. This internal dialogue, in which consciousness is divided in two, where one speaks in his own voice and the other in the voice he believes to be Vicente's, will carry on until the next death.

DIALOGUE II

Samson Flexor

§ Approximately one year before his death,
Flexor painted one's portrait. The painting is
predominantly light pink with a white background.
One's forehead and chin are filled in with thick oil
paint applied to the canvas and sculpted to look
worn away by time, like a geological formation – a
characteristic technique of Flexor's late period.
One's eyes are shaped differently: one a triangle,
the other an oval. The false symmetry of the face,
drawn as a curve suggesting an interrogation mark,
is stretched towards the bottom of the picture,
evoking a necktie in relief that dissolves vertically
into the background, creating a false perspective.
The title of the painting, "Dialogue," and the
signature are drawn in Flexor's characteristic
lettering, accentuating the "Fl" and the "r" shared
by our names. No one has ever offered a more
penetrating critique of one's *"being-in-the-world."*
There is also a portrait of Flexor on his deathbed,
which one's student photographed using a
phenomenological method one tried to bequeath to
a new generation of Brazilians: the portrait shows
him cleansed of quotidian detail and turned with
closed eyes towards the essence of life. The image
captures a definitive vision of Flexor's *"being-in-the
world"* and his *"no-longer-being-in-the-world."* Flexor
was not only revolutionary in the field of Brazilian

visual arts, but also revolutionary in relation to art and humanity as a whole. He was a curious sort of revolutionary, though: a noble man who sought to defeat bourgeois attitudes.

§ One had always felt a certain discomfort with the inconsistency in the Marxist concept of revolution: on the one hand it is a process through which the contradictions of reality's foundational structure synthetically overcome one another, but on the other hand, it is a process through which subjectivities become objective by projecting themselves onto reality. This inconsistency does not necessarily reveal itself on the theoretical level. On the contrary: at this level the double view of the revolution is profound. One can give three examples. Let us suppose that hydrogen is reality's simplest structure. Hydrogen has a complex internal contradiction between electrical charges and between the nucleus and the electron. There is also a complex external contradiction between the several atoms, for example there are several magnetic fields. The revolution is the synthetic leap from these contradictions onto a new level as helium emerges. The same process may be observed from a different perspective: from the hydrogen's point of view the creation of helium seems so improbable that it is impossible. However, hydrogen's internal and external contradictions make helium's appearance necessary. Therefore, helium is hydrogen's "impossible dream," and is, in this sense, a subjective projection. Let us suppose that amino acids are life's simplest structure. Amino acids have a complex internal contradiction, with electrical, chemical, and other types of instabilities. There is also an extremely complex external contradiction between the various molecules. The revolution is the synthetic leap from these contradictions to a new level where the living cell emerges. The same process may be observed from a different perspective: from the amino acids' point of view, the cell seems improbable to the point of being impossible. Therefore, the cell is the amino acids' "subjective dream" made real by overcoming their contradictions through revolution. Lets us suppose that to gather wild roots and fruits is economy's simplest structure. Gathering has a complex internal contradiction between the sexes and the different generations of the horde. There are also complex external contradictions between the different hordes; between the hordes and the forest; between the hordes and the climate. The revolution is the synthetic leap from these contradictions to a new level where the hunt emerges. The same process may be seen from a different perspective: from the gatherer's point of view the emergence of the hunter seems improbable to the point of being impossible. However, the gatherer "subjectively dreams" of becoming a hunter, and this dream becomes necessarily objective by overcoming the contradictions of the gatherer's structure through revolution. At this level of speculation there is no inconsistency in the Marxist view. Reality is a process of permanent revolution, and at every level of the process the subsequent level manifests itself as purely subjective, as an impossible dream.

§ However, inconsistency is revealed at the level of lived experience and praxis. The internal and external contradictions of the reality one lives may be objectively diagnosed – according to the Marxist model – as a process that necessarily seeks to give birth to a new level of reality through revolutionary methods; a level that can only be subjectively imagined and within these dreams may acquire a type of colouring that is political, economic, aesthetic, or religious. However, according to the Marxist model, there simultaneously exists an underlying infrastructure to reality at every level of the process (currently economic and social), and dreams remain alienated (in other words: disconnected from the revolutionary leap to be performed) if they do not project themselves over such an infrastructure. This is almost as if hydrogen dreamt of becoming a hunter, or the gatherer dreamt of becoming a living cell. This is madness. This is where the inconsistency lies. Because, on the one hand, it encourages a dream. But on the other, it discriminates between types of dreams. This inconsistency is undoubtedly the proof of Marxist sincerity. It is not a closed model that seeks to impose itself upon reality; it is an open model that accepts its own contradiction with reality. This would be a revolutionary model. However, the consequence of this inconsistency upon lived experience and praxis is the following:

the more one sincerely identifies with the Marxist model in theory, the farther one distances oneself from Marxist revolutionary praxis – both in one's experience of reality and in one's engagement as a whole. This becomes even clearer in relation to the field of the arts.

§ According to the Marxist definition, the artist projects his or her dreams onto reality, and he or she will be an *avant-garde* artist if those dreams subvert reality's infrastructure, instigating a revolutionary leap. In this sense the artist is like an organ that establishes a new reality for humanity. (At this point it is important to mention how Marxist Vargas is, even though he would never admit it.) However, after conceiving reality as a revolutionary process to overcome infrastructures, Marxism loses art's essence, which it still ascribes a decisive role: because Marxism limits aesthetic action to the field of infrastructure (doing so very indirectly). Truly "engaged" art does not necessarily have to be propaganda, and "socialist realism" is a Stalinist absurdity. For example, art can also be formal: Russian Formalism of the 1920s (so highly original) proves it. By dreaming and proposing new forms, the artist indirectly influences formally ossified infrastructures. Nevertheless, the aesthetic criterion continues to be engagement, a criterion artistic praxis does not accept, particularly if the artist is a Marxist. This is because in such cases the dialectic the artist must face is not the one between dream and reality's infrastructure, but the dialectic between the dream's pleasure and the resistance of matter (which is experienced as a challenge, therefore, with equal pleasure) – and of a type of matter that bears almost no relation to the infrastructure of reality. In other words: if the artist is really revolutionary, he or she will accept what is given and not seek to subvert the social and economic structures, but will aim at the structures of paint or words. The artist may subsequently attempt to objectify his or her engagement and say that subversion of the medium will influence infrastructures. However, this rationalisation will always be external to his or her true engagement. Therefore, according to the Marxist definition, the Marxist artist is an alienated artist. This may not be a theoretical contradiction and might be resolved within Marxist theory. However, existentially speaking, this is an insoluble contradiction – especially if the artistic engagement happens within a reality such as Brazil, which cries out for engagement with its infrastructures. If one aims at Brazilian infrastructures, one's dream is lost, and if one aims at one's dream, one becomes alienated from Brazilian reality. The Marxist model thus re-articulates the Hegelian contradiction: one either finds oneself and loses the world, or one engages with the world and loses oneself. There is no synthesis at the level of lived experience and praxis, and there is no synthesis *a fortiori* in a reality as provoking as Brazil. This was essentially the majority of one's dialogue with Flexor. It was a terrible subject, because the incongruence between vocation and responsibility within different types of existence, such as one's own and his, was constantly making itself evident.

§ There was no coincidence in the problem's coordinates, in the cases of both his and one's own situation. One was not an artist but a teacher and essayist. One's dreams were not visions but doubts, and these doubts, when communicated, reached the infrastructures, although indirectly and slowly. One did not have the same violent contradiction as Flexor. He subverted Brazilian art as a painter and teacher, thus powerfully contributing to the alienation of a whole group of people highly active in the infrastructure of Brazilian reality. In the end, however, the problem was the same, because the doubts one communicated had a tendency to paralyze action rather than encourage it. As Kant says: doubt is a necessary place of rest but not a place for dwelling. One was therefore an alienating factor within the Brazilian context. The subject of one's dialogue with Flexor – the sterility of authentic engagement with the dream and the repulsive inauthenticity of an engagement with Brazilian reality – which, based on his own prophecy, eventually "killed" Guimarães Rosa – was therefore a theme that relates to the artist's situation in an underdeveloped context, as well as every intellectual.

§ For a better understanding of this subject, the influence of our dialogue upon Flexor as he stood before a canvas may serve as a starting point. Flexor came to Brazil, soon after the war, burdened with conflicting traditions. On one side, he carried with him a solid Marxist grounding, which was responsible for him never using non-Marxist categories in his aesthetic analyses, and for our dialogue always moving within these categories. On the other side, Flexor carried with him the tradition of the Parisian school of painting (especially Cubism and Abstraction), a wide musical culture, an extraordinary intuition, and a penetrating knowledge of French and Russian poetry, beginning with the early twentieth century. There was also a more decisive element: Flexor was a graduate in mathematics, and this *forma mentis* was the climate in which his mind worked. From a strictly Platonic viewpoint, Flexor united within him *musike kai mathematike techne*, which means that Plato's objections to art did not apply to him. Once Flexor collided with Brazilian reality, his Marxist grounding served not only to grasp that reality, but fuelled his decision to engage with it. His engagement took two characteristically opposite paths: on the one hand Flexor founded the "abstraction studio" in order to introduce the Brazilian bourgeoisie to an active current of contemporary art, and on the other hand, he abandoned abstraction in his own canvases, opting for a geometric figuration that would communicate a revolutionary message to the masses. His analysis of the Brazilian reality convinced him that, for the masses, the most powerfully obscuring ideology was Catholicism,

Vilém Flusser

and he chose Catholic themes for his canvases to reveal the misery of Brazilian reality. Whenever possible, he used churches as the channels for his message. However, he noticed very early on that his own interest in such a project lay not in its message (the semantic aspect), but in the geometric structure (the syntactic aspect) and the play of colours. Hence, he gradually understood that the figurative aspect of the canvas distracted the viewer's attention from what was essential. In order to save his own authenticity as a painter, he abandoned the figure and with it his engagement with Brazilian reality. From that point on he painted mathematical equations in an effort to visualise the *aistheton* of advanced arithmetics. This meant a visual musicalisation of formal thought, which was already apparent in his religious paintings. Little by little the stress transferred from form (line and plane) to colour and his thought gained body and gradually became concrete. Effectively: Flexor was one of the first Concretists.

§ Then came a violent crisis. On the one hand, the deadly illness that advanced mercilessly and slowly engulfed Flexor, and his familiarity with death, triggered a growing distrust in the legitimacy of thought. On the other hand, our dialogues, and dialogues with those around us, opened for him a new view into the abyss. Flexor simultaneously experienced the Marquis de Sade's impact. For Flexor, he injected a libidinous dimension to the revolutionary attitude and aestheticised, in a certain way, Marxism. In Flexor's opinion, the artist today should play the same role Sade did in relation to the French Revolution – which Marcuse intellectually reinterpreted, weakly, in relation to the Russian Revolution. Thus, Flexor reformulated his attitude before the canvas. He returned to a negative figuration: not to paint things, but to paint the sadist nothingness behind things (the "Devil"). Thematically, this path was similar to F. Bacon's. However, it was technically different. Bacon sought to capture phenomenologically this gesture in its brutal absurdity. Flexor sought to capture ontologically the groundlessness in everything. He sought to capture nothingness as the ground for things, but above all, death as the ground for life. Since he continued essentially to be a Marxist, and for him "Being" meant "becoming," the best method was to progress in the opposite direction and paint "non-becoming." This meant, to paint the animal behind the human, the mineral behind the animal, and the abyss of nothingness behind the mineral. This was the genesis of his "monsters."

§ His aim required two convergent routes of attack: capturing an ephemeral vision of the decadence behind any type of *development*, which necessitated the use of watercolours; and fixing the sclerosed crystallisation of the decadence behind any type of *development*, for which oils on gigantic canvasses were necessary. The methods converged. A large series of watercolours accrued, which were variations on a single subject that became larger as the series progressed, gradually losing its impressionistic character as it moved towards monumentality. Monumental oil paintings simultaneously emerged, convergent to the watercolours. Each method demanded a different technique. The watercolours were a struggle against colour, aimed at the pink of anaemic blood and the white of hospital sterility and death. The oils were a struggle against paint, aimed at sculpting and digging hole of nothingness (which he called "openings"). Via these routes, Flexor became one of the most important contemporary water-colourists and one of the most violent contemporary renovators of oil painting (and acrylic painting). The results were colossal monuments to Nothingness; monsters at the same time anthropomorphic, zoomorphic, and geomorphic, with holes dug out of their entrails, floating in subtle colours above a white background and casting plastic shadows when light was shed upon them. They remain terrifying and beautiful, like death and the human condition.

§ To dialogue with Flexor meant to dialogue with all of that (although, in a certain way, the monsters were answers Flexor had already sent us). One's portrait by Flexor (which he called "Dialogue") was proof of this. Flexor hence became one's mirror. One saw oneself in his monsters, not only in the way anyone recognises himself in these monsters, but unfortunately in the way one recognised one's own influence on Flexor. This was how Flexor managed to visualise (not to say "make palpable") his own and one's situation as intellectuals in a world "progressing" towards omnipotent apparatus, in an underdeveloped country striving to become *developed*. We are monsters because we search for our vocation (our "dream") in our own entrails, while the world around us crystallises as an apparatus. We are "Sadists" in the original sense of the term: driven by our alienating (crazy) pleasure to realise ourselves whilst seeking to violate the world with our dreams. This is why Flexor dedicated a whole series of monsters "*in memoriam* of the Marquis." And that is precisely why we have our beauty, despite being mortal and decadent; the beauty of the true human condition. "*Entschluss zum Tode*" (determined to die): this was the answer Flexor hurled at us, which contributed greatly to one's decision to disengage. It is a great pity Flexor did not live long enough to witness one's decision.

§ In the end, there was a curious convergence between Flexor and Vicente. Certainly, they came from incongruent worlds: Flexor from the abyss that separates "artistic vocation" from Marxist engagement and Vicente from the conviction that humans and things tend to look towards the future, which conceals their sacred sources. Both arrived, however, at the same result: going towards sources and against these tendencies. For Flexor, this decision took the form of a rebellion against "God," against the powers he called "paternalistic," which drive us towards progress (not only scientific and technological, but political, economic, and social, as well). In sum: to rebel against the establishment on both the left and right sides. Flexor became a Sadist – or rather, a rebellious aristocrat (a Marquis). Vicente had the same "Sadism," which was a rebellion against the transcendent. Both became revolutionaries when in reality they were both rebels (desperate revolutionaries). Perhaps both suffered a type of conversion just before dying, and the answer they gave us, although "true," was unacceptable. One had to seek another "opening," different from the one they located; an opening like Flexor's deathbed photograph. To live means to continue one's dialogue with both, and "to save oneself" means to save them. Flexor seemed to yearn for it. His painful sweetness in his final days reminded one of his monsters' sweetness in seeking salvation. It remains an unforgettable memory, and one's unavoidable task.

João Guimarães Rosa

§ From a certain perspective, the dialogue with Guimarães Rosa followed a complementary structure to one's dialogue with Bloch. However, it was Guimarães Rosa who threw himself at us whenever we came close, so that one could function as his merciless critic. There was a difference, though: in dialogues with Bloch, everything was a subject, not just one's own work. With Guimarães Rosa, there was only one subject: Guimarães Rosa.

This subject was broad enough to encompass a reasonable portion of the problems that preoccupied us. And Guimarães Rosa's work is actually close enough to one's own that the subject "Guimarães Rosa" was not too distant from one's own praxis. Even so, one must confess that Guimarães Rosa's egocentrism demanded a great deal of self-abnegation – a difficult task, given one's tendency to think of oneself as the centre of the universe. In the beginning, this structure (he, the sender of messages; one, the receiver) seemed logical, given the relative position of the two participants. He, the Ambassador seated behind a desk in Itamaraty Palace, surrounded by the glory of a somewhat internationally known writer. One, a visitor from São Paulo seated in a lower chair, a potential disseminator of the Rosean glory. However, this extreme structure changed rapidly. He, pacing around the room, stripped of his jovial nature and prone to crying. One, systematically piercing the Rosean bubble, despite always respectfully keeping one's distance, imposed by the presence of greatness, in order to reach with him the core of his suffering. This was an ambivalent experience: on the one hand, it was pleasurable because it exposed Guimarães Rosa's incredibly rich world; on the other, it painfully revealed his weakness and suffering, which were to a large extent one's own suffering. In the course of our exchange there were moments when our roles were reversed (whoever has psychoanalytic experience might see this as a classic occurrence) and Guimarães Rosa tried to save us (for example, teaching one to pray or relinquish one's disdain for money or fame). In reality, Guimarães Rosa was really trying to justify himself to us – and one resisted the role of judge that he projected on us. The atmosphere of our dialogues was always marked by Guimarães Rosa's extreme fragility, which was exactly the opposite of Vargas, who can be mercilessly attacked and still hold his ground. Guimarães Rosa nearly crumbled at unpredictable moments. To this day one cannot decide which type is more depressing: the vulnerable or resistant. The juxtaposition Rosa/Vargas proves that both types, when inhabited by creative personalities, can be very sensitive.

§ The grand subject "Guimarães Rosa" had four dimensions, which, despite mutual interference, stood out as our dialogue progressed. In ascending order, the dimensions were the following: (a) *Brazilianess*, as it manifested in the countryside of the State of Minas Gerais, (b) different global trends of the literary novel and Guimarães Rosa's impact on them, (c) the Portuguese language and language *tout court*, and (d) salvation of the soul.

§ This book presupposes that Brazilian readers know the work of Guimarães Rosa and, therefore understand the following: *Brazilianess* was the least important dimension for Guimarães Rosa; it acquired importance only when related to the other three dimensions. But it tends to be perceived by readers as the most important Rosean "message," which can have disastrous consequences. One consequence is that the universal quality of his oeuvre becomes obscured. This is a grave danger, given the enormous difficulty translating Guimarães Rosa into other languages. Guimarães Rosa could be easily transformed into another "regional author," which would be a caricature. The other disastrous consequence is that current events in Brazil are exactly the opposite of Guimarães Rosa's projected vision of "Brazilian essence," which means he could be transformed into "an old fashioned" or "nostalgic" artist, and this would be inappropriate. Once framed within "the history of literature" in the academy and in textbooks he would become innocuous, which would equate to castrating Guimarães Rosa — when in reality his work not only subverts language but thought through the subversion of language. One hopes this reminiscence of Guimarães Rosa serves, as a reminder of the fact he represented a revolution in Brazilian thought. He revealed a universally significant aspect of Brazil, although an aspect which so-called "developmentalism" tends to progressively eradicate.

§ In the course of our dialogue with Guimarães Rosa, the four previously mentioned dimensions of his oeuvre crystallised around four blocks: (a) The man from the countryside as prototype of a *unio mystica* between Man and nature in general, in a more or less Plotinian sense — which is something to be expanded upon because this typically Brazilian heritage represents one of the few routes available to human salvation, to avoid being profaned by massification. (b) The literary novel is currently in a crisis because it presupposes a universe where the author is omniscient and manipulates events – a universe that is unacceptable today. The salvation of the literary novel will only happen if the author becomes concretely (not just technically) one of the characters in its universe, as ignorant of his or her destiny as the other characters, and as prone to being manipulated by unknown and mysterious powers. (c) Language has the power to establish reality and comes before it in the same way that, "In the beginning was the Word." Language also precedes the poet, who does not create language but creates within and with language. Every language therefore imposes its specific reality upon the poet, who must seek to identify with the specificity of that language if she or he wants to participate in its creative process. This is *a fortiori* true in the case of the Portuguese language, whose essence is plasticity. (d) Today there is a confusion between two types of immortality: the immanent type as a result of creativity (to carry on living within others), which can be quantifiable (Guimarães Rosa is more immortal than his barber), or ontologically dubious (Riobaldo is more immortal that Guimarães Rosa); and the transcendent type, which is the only type of immortality that matters, existentially. One devours the other, which is the fundamental Rosean conviction.

§ One can easily see how the first three dimensions interfere with one another and end up eventually in the fourth dimension, and how Guimarães Rosa's tragedy (impressively demonstrated by his own death) was his conviction that his own immortality (famous author and member of the Brazilian Academy of Immortals) kills the immortality of the nameless "soul," which is what he was in the end. One does not exaggerate by saying that Guimarães Rosa "surrendered" – or rather, "surrendered his soul" – by becoming officially immortal in a way that was repugnant to him. Faith in an insurmountable dialectic between the immanent and the transcendent may seem like a nefarious superstition – until one infiltrates Rosean thought's core and this faith emerges diabolically as lucid and consistent. Let us therefore unfold the four dimensions of his thought to reveal the core and impact it had upon one's own thought and engagement.

§ (A) The fundamental human experience is to be thrown by unknown forces into the untrodden *Sertão* [backlands] of the world, and to travel aimlessly through it searching for salvation, which is death; a journey surrounded on all sides by temptation, traps ("unfounded pitfalls"), and a non-existent Devil. In his own words, this experience meant, "to live is very dangerous." What is terrifying is that, for us, who appear to be sheltered by history, numerous ideologies and the residue of the quotidian conceal this fundamental experience. Thanks to myths

9. Guimarães Rosa used the Portuguese term *estória* in the same manner as the English term **story**, in order to differentiate it from **história** or **history** because Portuguese does not have this differentiation. However, in his use of the term, he associated it with heroic and tragic narratives, instead of the common use, which is to denote folkloric narratives. I chose to translate it as **heroic** since a phonetic approximation in English as **storic** would not work.

10. **Nonanda** is the first word in Guimarães Rosa's masterpiece **Grande Sertão: Veredas**, first published in Brazil in 1956. **Nonada** is a neologism made up of two words, the preposition **no**. which translates as **in** and the noun **nada**. which translates as **nothing**, or **nothingness**.

like *The Odyssey, Exodus*, and the legend of *The Holy Grail*, we are only able to gaze at our condition like aimless travellers, and at our aimless journey as the search for an aim. In the Brazilian countryside, however – such as it was during Guimarães Rosa's youth – there were still people who experienced, concretely, the fundamental human condition. From one's own perspective, these people lived "mythically." Cowboys, *cangaceiros* [outlaws], and their "dames" were prehistoric nomads (in the radical sense of the term "history"); they were "heroic" [*estóricos*[9]] beings: uprooted from the world and in search of the Other. The mystery is that, in the course of their journey, they became confused with the world, precisely because they were rootless. They are non-historical because they have not been historicised; one can confuse them with the bull, the ass, the flower, and the palm-tree in their unconscious and mythical search for an "aim." They are not people ("masks"); they are existences or "in'nothing" [*nonada*[10]]. They are ambivalent characters (*Diadorims*[11]), who run in vain [*debalde*] (*Riobaldo*[12]), and who inhabit the third riverbank. They are real because they live in the fundamental human condition. This is the Rosean *Sertão*: the world of myth, which he experienced concretely as a child. And these are the Rosean *Veredas*: journeys in search of an aim. And this is the Rosean Brazilian countryside: the territory of human salvation, "utopia," a place that cannot be found on a map. This utopia exists in the memory of Brazilian people as a concrete reality, and must or even as **the void**. Translators have always had difficulty translating this word, mainly because many tend to miss its philosophical and existential meaning. When Guimarães Rosa says **nonada**, he literally means **in nothingness** or **in the void**, as in the existentialist notion of being thrown into meaningless existence, a meaningless world floating in a meaningless universe.

11. **Diadorim** is one of the main characters in **Grande Sertão: Veredas**, an outlaw woman living as a man among a band of outlaws.

12. **Riobaldo** is the protagonist of **Grande Sertão: Veredas**

13. **Niquites** is also a Rosean neologism, but Flusser uses it for its melodic quality as it sounds like the English **never quitting**.

be preserved. It is a way of "saving their souls." But it is a dangerous method. Because the Devil that does not exist and who powerfully manifests himself in Brazilian reality today is always ready (*Niquites*[13]) to devour them. This is Guimarães Rosa's "Brazilianist" message.

§ (B) The literary novel and the short story (as well as other "literary" forms) are late descendants of the *epos*: an inspired form of storytelling inspired by the Muses (*Odyssey*), by Jehovah (*Exodus*), or by the whispering of leaves (*Sagas*). The fact that the *epos* is inspired is manifested both in its message and its form. Its message is manifested in that the *epos* is the "telling of a myth" or events that take place in non-historical time, or a "heroic" [*estórico*] one, to use a Rosean term. Form is manifested in a slow, grand, poetic and highly connotative telling. As the West became historical, it distanced itself from its source of inspiration, from the *epos*, and the consequence was that the literary novel and the short story of the 19th-century (which represented the apex of distance from the source) became demythologised. The telling of events took place in a historical time frame (Tolstoy) and became de-poeticised, prosaic, nervous, concentrated, and denotative (Zola). Ontologically, what happened is that the author of the literary novel (and *a fortiori* of the American short story) turned himself into the source of inspiration, by taking on the perspective of the Divine Creator. The author played God and the result was "fiction," the universe of the literary

Vilém Flusser

novel as the author's projection onto historical reality – a projection in which the author only participated as a subject transcending that universe. In the beginning of the 20th century, this resulted as a crisis of the literary novel, when psychologising and socialisation – the scientification of the literary novel – made the contradiction between "realism" and the fictitious nature of its universe untenable. Two ingenious attempts to reformulate the literary novel emerged: Joyce's and Kafka's. Joyce's approach sought to recapture the authentic form of the *epos* through slow, grand, and highly connotative telling as a multi-layered stream of consciousness, which automatically redirected him to the sources of myth (*Finnegans Wake* is an example). Kafka sought to overcome the fictitious character of the literary novel by immersing the author in its universe (in the form of K.), which resulted in a new form of telling (a highly connotative witness account) and a new message (relative to non-historical events, although not mythical in the strictest sense of the term). Besides the historical West, however, there were always sources sprouting epics: Middle Eastern markets, Central African villages, and the countryside of the State of Minas Gerais in Brazil. Guimarães Rosa therefore found himself in a privileged situation, where he could simultaneously watch Joyce and Kafka's attempts to recreate the literary novel and experience the emergence of the *epos* in the countryside of the State of Minas Gerais. That slow, grand, and muddy monologue; the redneck's small and soft talk, with its labyrinthine turns and refrained repetitions, and the visions of a non-historical mythical world: these were the vehicles for the Minas Gerais' *epos*. If elevated to the level of Joyce and Kafka, this monologue could become a vehicle for a whole new Western *epos*. However, this could not be achieved through a kind of intellectual decision around types: one cup Minas Gerais, one cup Joyce, shake, and serve hot. The very character of the *epos* as an inspired tale excludes this type of decision. It was necessary to avoid that route. In other words: to delve into the mythic atmosphere of Minas Gerais and the post-historical atmosphere of Joyce and Kafka, allowing himself to be dominated by both – and only then become a spokesman for them. For Guimarães Rosa this was achieved spontaneously, since he was part of Minas Gerais from birth and of Joyce and Kafka's world by cultural tradition, social position, and conscious self-teaching. The Rosean *"estórias"* are therefore an epic synthesis of Minas Gerais monologue and the existential reformulation of the literary novel in relation to Guimarães Rosa's *being-in-the-world* – and not in relation to deliberate technique. Despite avoiding deliberate technique, however, the *estórias* call for a whole series of manipulations and tricks: internal and external refrain, deliberate social enumeration, deliberate counterpoint between intended and sub-intended meaning, and so on. Once the existential synthesis has been reached, technical problems become the focus; this was the subject of our dialogues and it generated an internal contradiction: his increasingly masterful technique threatened the authenticity and spontaneity of the prose, resulting in a kind of schizophrenia. On the one hand, his real "Self" was immersed in the *epos*, living and "travelling" within it; on the other was Guimarães Rosa the "great writer," increasingly masterful at perfectly manipulating the *epos* and therefore manipulating his real "Self." The writer's "soul" devoured Guimarães Rosa's real one until the Brazilian Academy of Letters tragically crowned this anthropophagic banquet. "Art," or rather artifice, artfulness, and lie triumphed over truth.

§ (C) One had published a book titled *Language and Reality*,[14] which had moved one reader to the core: Guimarães Rosa. The thesis in the book is that language is not only a map of the world (essentially Wittgensteinian), but also that it projects worlds and enters into a feedback with what is projected. According to this thesis, the function of language is not limited to the ontological and epistemological aspects of language but, on the contrary, is dominated by the aesthetic aspects of language. This thesis, which one had not developed speculatively but had lived through one's practical experience in thinking and writing, coincided with Guimarães Rosa's, and made him aware of so much that had, until then, lain in the penumbra of subliminality. One's book was the pretext for the dialogues with Guimarães Rosa: we purportedly spoke about the book. In reality, however, we spoke about Guimarães Rosa. The fact that we

14. Flusser, V. **Lingua e Realidade**. Herder, São Paulo 1964.

experienced the *aistheton* of language differently from each other was clear to both of us. In one's opinion, any phenomenology of language must start from spoken rhythm and the visual *Gestalt* of written language. For Guimarães Rosa (who was never really a writer but a storyteller — *vates*), the visual *Gestalt* was secondary and the melody of spoken language fascinated him. Curiously, however, as Guimarães Rosa's *oeuvre* progressed, he became a revolutionary of the Brazilian *Gestalt*, and the Concretists and other practitioners emerged from his groundwork. If one had any impact on Brazilian thought, it was not through the reformulation of writing's *Gestalt* — and one's rhythmic preoccupations unfortunately went largely unnoticed. *Habent fata libelli*. Guimarães Rosa's musical inebriation — his obsession with the letter "a", for instance, or the hypnotizing effect that the diminutive form "-*im*" had on him, or his constant onomatopoeia — was excessively sweet because it seemed like abandoning himself to the melodic essence of Portuguese. In one's view, the Rosean neologisms (so admired by his critics) were ambivalent and dangerously close to facile word games, for this reason: Guimarães Rosa embodied the essence of Portuguese, but he had a vast knowledge of several other languages, too. His knowledge was wide, however, but not deep and his neologisms, although perfectly adequate in Portuguese, only rubbed the surface in which a profound mystery vibrates. A single word serves as an apt example: *Sagarana*. The word "sounds" Portuguese-ish and can be easily located within

Portuguese syntax. It has the melody of the letter "a," so feverishly loved, and thus evokes Sanskrit, with all its mysterious connotations. But the lower German word *"Saga"* (vaguely, "myth") has an inexhaustible richness that Guimarães Rosas misses, and the Tupi suffix *"-rana"* suggests an agglutinative plural, which is also lost. What remains is only a pretty way of saying "several myths." Behind this neologism lies a type of intellectual deliberation that leaves, despite the sweetness, a bad taste in the mouth. Conversely, the ruptured syntax Guimarães Rosa managed to achieve and the ingenious way he pushed discourse to absurdity (for example, in his perfect short story "My Uncle the Jaguar") — and his wise use of the sentence against the word and the word against the sentence — make it seem as if Portuguese became self-conscious and turned against itself. In this respect, Guimarães Rosa pointed the way towards a new universe.

§ Leaving these differences aside, we fundamentally agreed that language is not "a communication medium," but that it is the very foundation of Being, in which logos = *mythos*. For both of us, to write — although it implies communication with others — is the only method for realising our own essences (the language that lies silent within us). This silent language exerts pressure and seeks violently to become the written word — a Husserlian *"zum Worte kommen."* Thus, one's own writing practice emerges as an existential unification of Wittgenstein and Husserl. Guimarães Rosa's practice emerged the same way, although with different terminology, attempting to existentially unify *logos* and *mythos*. The logic of myth and the mythical dimension of logic are the climate of Rosean writing. However, the diabolic dichotomy churning up Guimarães Rosa's entrails also manifests itself with murderous virulence in his writing.

§ To write means to work above language but also within it. The practice of writing implies a constant distancing from language – for example, in the form of word lists kept in desk drawers, disciplined study of country slang, or grammatical examination of other languages. In turn, this self-distancing alienated Guimarães Rosa from the language that sprang silently from his own *being-in-the-world*. Guimarães Rosa the linguist, who became increasingly masterful, killed Guimarães Rosa the "*vates*." There was no sense in comparing this diabolical vision to one's own practice: the linguist provoked the "*vates*" just as the "*vates*" provoked the linguist, through mutual reciprocation. Guimarães Rosa felt desperately that he was becoming too technical, and the irony of his last book *Primeiras Estórias* [First Stories] is that it is a purely technical attempt to incorporate an alienating technical approach. Furthermore, as his techniques became more "popular" and were adopted by other writers, they became progressively less-Rosean (reified). But Guimarães Rosa could not abandon them without abandoning himself. In developing these techniques and communicating them to society, Guimarães

Rosa had "sold his truly immortal soul" to Brazil. His acceptance into the Brazilian Academy of Letters proved it. There was no way out, except the heart attack that killed him.

§ (D) The dichotomy of "immortality in the immanent/immortality in the transcendent," which one saw as "engagement/self-absorption," and which permeated all of Guimarães Rosa's activities, became for him entirely depoliticised. This never had the same meaning for Guimarães Rosa as it did for Flexor. For Flexor, this meant the impossible choice of either engaging in the fundamental Brazilian reality or becoming a real artist. For Guimarães Rosa, being a writer meant engaging in the fundamental Brazilian reality (which is mythical and, therefore, linguistic), and the impossible choice was between either being a writer or "truly" Being. One always found it amusing and disquieting to observe how much Guimarães Rosa identified his work as a writer with "engaging in favour of and against Brazilian reality," and how much he identified himself with "Brazil." This egocentrism (reminiscent of Goethe's identification with Germany and Unamuno's with Spain) was disturbing, especially from someone who functioned as a significant expression of a given reality (but who obviously could not be identified with it). It posited an ethical problem such that even Guimarães Rosa could not accept it. From his perspective, Flexor's dilemma (and any other intellectual in an underdeveloped context) is superficial because engagement both with social reality and art means alienation from the only reality that really matters: the transcendent soul. For Flexor, however – and a large number of leftist intellectuals and Catholics – Guimarães Rosa's dilemma was entirely superficial because his engagement with art and his introspective search for salvation meant alienation from the only reality that mattered: achieving salvation through actively loving the Other. Whenever one attempted to point this out to Guimarães Rosa (in order to show a different perspective), he became so upset one had to cease discussing the problem immediately. There was something inside Guimarães Rosa (perhaps his creative force) that blocked his view of the world, when he was not the central focus.

§ The fact was, Guimarães Rosa was sovereignly indifferent (and here the term "sovereignly" applies perfectly) to the Brazilian geographical and historical reality, just as he was indifferent to the geographical and historical reality of the world beyond Brazil. He was "above" all of it, which was ethically a very dubious place. He had his own "Brazil" (a mythical utopia) and his own world (the world of languages). These were the fields on which he acted, thereby endangering the immortality of his own soul. Suddenly, however, a significant contradiction emerged. His engagement in these worlds of his own creation demanded collaboration with others – which inevitably pointed towards the centre of the world, which was Guimarães

Rosa. The others were there only inasmuch as they were Guimarães Rosa's readers, critics, translators, illustrators, or editors. This suggests that Guimarães Rosa used others to project himself into their worlds when in fact the opposite was true: he depended desperately on others. Guimarães Rosa was so fragile he lived in constant fear of others. Any negative criticism, no matter how benign or how obscure the critic, hurt him deeply. And any praise, no matter how superficial, comforted him. He had no distance from his work; he had no criteria to judge it – a surprising fact for someone who could muster so much technical distance to produce the work. He absorbed absolutely everything. The worst translations of his work excited him. If one pointed out the terrible mistakes made in the German translation and suggested changes, Guimarães Rosa became deeply disturbed. There was no better critic of the film based on one of his stories than himself. He avidly collected any scrap of printed matter with his name on it. He feared being "forgotten," but was unafraid of being abused. He published anywhere. He desperately sought to become "famous." And he always expected to be paid well, because for him money was the measure of fame.

§ This was the opposite of vanity, however. It was a kind of speculation *à la baisse* in the stock exchange of salvation, in the same way Thomas Mann described it in *Doktor Faustus*. He wanted to sell his immortal soul for the highest price, in order to reach salvation from the inside out. Fame was the same as the Devil that does not exist, and he knew very well that fame does not exist. The problem of translation perfectly illustrates this. One watched, in a kind of negative way, how he collaborated on the Mayer-Classon translation to German and on the Bizzarri translation to Italian. Fundamentally, Guimarães Rosa is untranslatable, because he *is* the Portuguese language, revolting against itself.

§ He is translatable at the semantic level, but only in relation to the superficial meaning of his words. These translations resulted in reproductions of Guimarães Rosa's anecdotes, offering the reader an entirely inaccurate view of Guimarães Rosa (as a kind of tropicalizing and exotic regionalist). It is possible, however, to recreate Guimarães Rosa within a different language. For example, the title *Grande Sertão: Veredas* could be translated to Rosean-like German as *Grosses Holz & Holzwege*. Bizzarri worked towards this idea in Italian, but Mayer-Classon abandoned the task. Guimarães Rosa knew this and one did not try to point it out to him. It did not matter to him. What mattered was to become "well-known" around the world.

§ He travelled to Germany to watch his book launch, although he knew the translation betrayed his *magnum opus*. In his view, the translation for the North American market, which was titled *The Devil to Pay in the Backlands* and threatened to turn him into a kind of storyteller about cowboys, was better than no translation. If Hollywood had made a film with *Diadorim* played by Marilyn Monroe, he would have been thrilled. This was fame at any cost, because it cost his soul.

§ A dialogue with such a giant, with such gigantic problems, could only undermine the foundation of one's own thought and engagement. There was a great temptation to use Guimarães Rosa as a springboard for projecting one's own "fame," in the Rosean sense. He wrote two short stories for us in a codified form, which were published in the *Literary Supplement* of the *O Estado de São Paulo* newspaper alongside one's commentary. One was titled *The Crane* and was perfectly convincing. One would only have to continue this public collaboration to become famous. Thankfully, one resisted, because Guimarães Rosa was living proof of the idea of fame — not only in the Rosean sense, where fame kills immortality (an idea which one hardly managed to accept with sincerity), but also in two additional ways. The first is that the aim of engagement is to change oneself by changing the world, which means "to open oneself towards the other" — and fame is nothing but a correlate (intrinsically indifferent) to engagement. The second is that, to chase fame cannot mean the loss of immortality but it means the definitive loss of the only kind of happiness one has ever known: disengaged work. Suddenly, a suspicion emerges that could become a provisional diagnosis of Guimarães Rosa: whenever he worked (one had witnessed this several times), an aura of creative happiness pervaded the room. But when he emerged from the work, there was a sensation of incomprehensible humiliation. Guimarães Rosa read what he had just written, praising each word and defending himself from an invisible critic. There was no use in telling him that the text was beautiful (and it was, most of the time, extremely beautiful), because his invisible critic remained intractable and refused comment. For him, this critic signified "the immortality of the soul." He exhibited an extremely curious type of Plotinism; a bleeding demiurge. However, there was no Plotinism in Guimarães Rosa, but a merciless Manichaeism — except that he was not a Christian. He had the humility of *hubris* whereas Vicente had the *hubris* of humility. Guimarães Rosa's "soul" was a de-Christianised *pneuma*, and this was the fundamental subject of his work: a *pneuma* he knew to be the Devil. Perhaps this is the ultimate Brazilian problem, a barely superficial Christianised Manichaeism. Guimarães Rosa was, therefore, the ultimate expression of Brazilian essence through his type of beauty. This was what one was forced to digest in some form, but one's subsequent life proved it was indigestible.

Haroldo de Campos

§ The dialectic between rational and irrational assumes different forms. For Vargas, it is between engineering and ontology. For Vicente it was between formal logic and the uncovering of Being. For Flexor, it was between political engagement and art. And for Guimarães Rosa, it was between writing and praying. For Haroldo de Campos, it is between deliberation and spontaneity. When he was invited by Max Bense to publish a portion of his *Galáxias* [Galaxies] in the *Rotehefte* in Stuttgart, Campos asked us to translate two excerpts from the text in German. This was a challenge that allowed one not only to delve into Campos' oeuvre, but also to activate and manipulate it. The operative contradiction within Campos subsequently became operative within us and exposed its dilemma. *Galáxias* is a series of variations on a few themes, executed in words chosen *ad hoc*, for example, the words *book* and *travel*. These variations occur on at least three levels: the phonetic *Gestalt*, in which the word's theme is gradually varied to activate its sound; the visual *Gestalt*, in which letters are varied within the word's structure; and semantic charge, in which the word's most varied connotations are gradually evoked. A syntactically unstructured discourse emerges from this, an uninterrupted flow of words in several different languages and neologisms reminiscent of "word associations" and "stream of consciousness" – with a countering flow that is solidly structured by the suggested verbal themes. The *Galáxias* are composed of circular discourse-flows: each individual discourse returns to the initial theme, creating a circular system in which satellite systems circulate and the focus is on words undergoing variation – hence the title

Galáxias. These galaxies spin within the universe of the Portuguese language, which serves as an infrastructure. But they constantly disrupt this infrastructure and expand towards the universes of other languages and non-languages. They also pulsate at certain points, causing the language to condense and form new "star-words" or, at other points, dissolve into nebulous, cosmic dust.

§ The problem for Campos is not on the level of theme. This choice is deliberately random and the contradiction between what is deliberate and accidental, between dice and chance, is a conscious starting point. In this sense, Campos is responding to Mallarmé, and there *is* no problem. However, what happens is that the theme proposed by a chosen word induces on the three previously mentioned levels a spontaneous current of variations that flows intensely and uncontrollably in a particular direction. And instead of surrendering to this current, Campos tries to divert it towards his brand of political engagement – and whenever the current is in danger of drying up, he deliberately tries to give it a series of nudges. The result is an ill feeling on the part of whoever receives the message. Campos has two options: he can either try to communicate a specific message, in which case the spontaneous flow of variations is not the best choice, or he can attempt to experiment concretely with the Portuguese language, in which case the deliberate manipulation of the flow falsifies the result. One cannot have one's cake and eat it, too.

Vilém Flusser

§ In trying to translate into German two of the circular discourses that make up his galaxies, this negative dialectic became painfully clear: if one chose the German words equivalent to the ones used by Campos, the current of variations was automatically (effectively: imperiously) produced. The current emerged with such vehemence that it was necessary to prune it. At which point, one realised that to prune it did not mean either to direct or nudge it, but to channel it. This meant "saving the resulting intuition" in Occam's sense: *entia non sunt multiplicanda praeter necessitatem* (elements must not be multiplied unnecessarily). However, it did not mean that he imposed his will on the current. Thus, the places where Campos interfered externally upon his texts in order to pervert them became obvious. The effect was the exact opposite of what he intended. The "ideological" message that emerged sounded artificial and false, and his nudges to the flow did not result in highlighting the flow's strength, but its weakness. In the translation, this curtailed one's own spontaneity.

§ This negative dialectic relates not only to Campos' engagement with poetry but in a more profound way to any type of engagement in any field of art. Undoubtedly, the dialectic between spontaneity and deliberation is the price we must pay for our loss of innocence. As we *do* something, we know *what* we are doing, *how* we are doing it, and, within certain limits, even know *why* and *for what* we are doing it. This distance from one's own practice exerts an influence on it. A constant feedback between praxis and "theory" emerges (in this case "theory" encompasses ideologies), and this feedback is tacked onto the feedback between practice and medium (in Campos' case, the Portuguese language). These interfering dialectics demand clear positioning: one either accepts the dialectic between theory and praxis or the practitioner's internal dialectic between the act of doing and the object's resistance. One cannot assume both positions because one negates the other (this is an aspect of the dialectic of consciousness and of the human condition). If one assumes the first position, one starts to engage in the translation of theory through practice – hence, one becomes "political" in the Platonic sense of the term. If one assumes the second position, one engages against one's medium, hence becoming an "artist" in the concrete sense of the term. Clearly, one position implies the other, but in a hierarchical manner: if one assumes the first position, one's "political" engagement will be a meta-engagement and one's artistic practice its object. If one assumes the second position, one's artistic engagement will be a meta-engagement and one's "theory" its substratum, pushed to the horizon. If one assumes both positions, one is neither "political" nor "concrete."

§ This inevitable existential decision has an ontological component: one must decide "one's" reality. In other words, one must decide which will be the object one seeks to subvert and alter in order to subvert and alter oneself. In the first case "one's" reality will be that towards which one's theory points (e.g., the infrastructures of the society that shelters one). In the second case, "one's" reality will be what one's praxis points towards (for example, the Portuguese language). The attempt to assume both positions will result in an ontological confusion that will be mirrored inevitably in the work. Such is Campos' problem (and anyone else who, even honestly, wishes to obviate a choice imposed by the human condition).

§ For Flexor, the necessity of making a choice was clear and he accepted it with great suffering, becoming a great painter and ending up alienated from what was, according to his idea, Brazilian reality. For Campos, the choice does not seem inevitable and the image of "the engaged artist" appears to be a possibility. That is why he suffers less than Flexor — although it is his art that suffers. This is a shame, both from the perspective of those who expect efficient action in the field of "politics" and those who expect from him efficient action in the field of language. For the first group, it seems obvious that his method of subverting syntax is not a very efficient way for subverting the infrastructures of reality. For the second group, the deliberate introduction of theory and ideology into linguistic practice destroys its concreteness.

§ In the dialogues with Campos, one consistently assumed the second position. This was not only because one's own interest was passionately focused on linguistic practice – and therefore saw Campos in parallel engagement – but also because one shared Flexor's conviction that, in certain contexts, any "political" engagement demands full commitment (including, among other things, the abandonment of artistic practice), which is impossible without abandoning one's vocation (something one was incapable of doing). Campos interpreted one's position not as a challenge but as the articulation of one's own "political" and artistic alienation (according to his definition of the term). For Campos, one's own position in relation to him (and, therefore, the "world") was like a cloud hovering over him, closing himself off to his own dilemma. The consequence was that he turned away from us, which one always lamented – both out of egoism and because of Campos' *oeuvre*.

§ There is no doubt that Campos' view of the problem of writing today, and specifically of writing in Portuguese, is fundamentally correct. This means accepting that to write means both drawing on a plane as well as transcribing the audible flow, which is a signifying code. It also means accepting that to write in Portuguese means to act upon a syntactically rigid but semantically open language. Campos undoubtedly achieves impressive results in his writing (as well as the "Concretists" who work with him). *Galáxias* is only one example. Among the most important results, the "Concretist" experiments raised awareness in relation to the *Gestalt* of writing, or the visual character of letters; the possibility of combining letters and non-letters; problems of pagination; and inserting pages into new contexts. This new awareness infiltrated not only the general press and book design field but also, perhaps more significantly, poster design and subsequently urban space. This meant a reformulation of clogged up channels (from Gutenberg's galaxies) in order to transmit new types of messages. Concretist experiments are rupturing discursive thought and endowing it with a second dimension of "ideas" which discursive thought cannot supply. In this sense, the Concretists wisely apply models provided by ideographic Eastern writing and combinations of writing, such as Japanese *haiku*. These models infiltrate Brazilian concrete poetry directly (thanks to the presence of Japanese and Chinese persons in Brazil) and indirectly (thanks to, for example, E. Pound), but they undergo an important reformulation. The Concretists' experiments make full use of information theory, playing creatively with noise and redundancies on the level of letters, words, and meaning. This adds to these texts an informative charge that is almost new to Brazilian literature. The Concretists' experiments allow for new translation techniques (for example, Joyce and the Russian Formalists), which were previously untranslatable. They also allow for the analysis of Brazilian texts (those of Oswald de Andrade and

Guimarães Rosa, for instance), which traditional interpretation methods did not. These are but a few examples, but there is no doubt that it is a very important movement for Brazilian literature – and, consequently, for Brazilian culture.

§ The issue stated at the beginning of this chapter problematises the whole movement, however. Perhaps one could radically reformulate it in the following manner: there is no doubt that a poem (or any other text) is not composed of either ideas or sentiments, but of words – as long as the term "word" is conceived concretely as a visual and audible *Gestalt* and meaningful symbol. However, there is also no doubt that the word is a mysterious phenomenon that reveals and conceals Being, and which must be approached with almost religious reverence. The word is both *logos* and *mythos*. The Concretists dilemma means that they "manipulate" the word, or they treat it as mediation but do not "accept" it phenomenologically with all of its mysterious charge. It is as if the Concretists (specially Haroldo de Campos) did not allow themselves the "luxury" of being awestruck by the mystery of the word. In this sense, they are the opposite of Guimarães Rosa, who fell victim of the mysterious power of words. That is why Guimarães Rosa is a powerful poet. To reformulate: in taking on the dialectic between theory (and ideology) and praxis, the Concretists cannot adopt the dialectic between producing texts and the mystery of words, which is the object of such praxis. The late Mayakovski and Yesenin (translated perfectly into Portuguese by a team of Concretists) should have shown them why it is necessary to adopt the mystery of words as the object of praxis. If they did not learn this, it must be because Campos' position is a rigid one (dogmatic) – always a dangerous thing for productivity.

§ One's dialogue with Campos continues unilaterally, as what I have just written proves. One continues to be fascinated by the Concretist movement, not so much in its realisation as its potentiality. The movement has two main currents, one represented by Décio Pignatari and the other by Pedro Xisto, with the Campos brothers in the middle. The Pignatari current aims towards informatics and the Xisto current towards an Eastern phenomenology of the word. Perhaps there is an internal contradiction within the movement that may be overcome synthetically by leaping to the next level: a truly new poetry. If Campos is seen as a precursor, he becomes incredibly relevant in the context of Brazilian poetry. One seeks and shall continue to seek being useful in helping him realise such a leap, even though, until now, he has refused the offer.

Dora Ferreira da Silva

§ Before anything can be stated about one's dialogues with Dora, a methodological problem arises. The Other's concrete presence imposes itself in two ways: mediately and immediately. Mediately, this presence imposes itself in the artwork through which the other communicates. Immediately, this presence imposes itself through the heat of shared existence and mutual openness. When the other is a creative person (someone who produces), this duplicity is not generally experienced as a problem: the work is an integral part of the living dialogue.

§ This was the case in one's dialogues with Flexor and Guimarães Rosa: their oeuvre was present in the dialogue. One always saw Flexor as his monster *Justino* and Guimarães Rosa as his character *Riobaldo*. To accept Flexor meant to accept his oils, as he was not Flexor without them. To accept Guimarães Rosa meant to accept *Tatuméia*, as he was not Guimarães Rosa without her. However, for some mysterious reasons, the same was not true with Dora. One is not suggesting that there is a rupture between Dora's work and her *being-in-the-world*. On the contrary: her poetry vibrates in tune with her palpitating existence, and her works on theory and philosophy betray the problems of her concrete view of the world. Perhaps the rupture lies within oneself: from one's perspective, Dora's concrete presence emanates a climate different from the one emanating from her work. Her poetry emanates the beauty of harmony, while her concrete presence emanates the beauty of suffered dissonance. Beauty is the common element in both climates and Dora is Beauty present (together with all the ethical problems implied). Two explications of this rupture (which are probably subjective): Dora either articulates in her *oeuvre* only one dimension of her Being, or she synthesises in her *oeuvre* the disagreement that lies at the root of her *being-in-the-world*. In any case, a deep critique of her poetry (which must be done in order to grasp the Brazilian situation) will prove that neither psychological nor biographical approaches are entirely satisfactory to phenomenologically grasp art. Dora, as a living person, does not "explain" her poetry, so the hypothesis of a trans-subjective inspiration seems unavoidable.

§ This is disturbing, because it implies that Dora is a poet despite herself. Flexor's "art/engagement" Guimarães Rosa's "art/prayer," and Campos' "spontaneity/deliberation" are the dilemmas of those who need to choose, who are condemned to freedom. They are not Dora's dilemmas. Dora is not free *to be* a poet but she is only free *as* a poet. For her, art *is* engagement and prayer and deliberation *are* spontaneity. Dora cannot comprehend the others' dilemmas, even at the level of poetry. This suggests a simplistic (Romantic) conclusion: that Dora's is authentic poetry and the others cannot reach such a level of radical authenticity. Unfortunately, concrete reality is not so Romantic and simple, because the term "authenticity" implies that contemporary Man (he who is condemned to accept himself as subject, to speak from a Marxist perspective) is distanced from himself, which includes being distant from the "intuition" that possesses him. Our virginity has been definitely lost.

§ This requires a word of caution. Dora's poetry is not in any way naive, as the preceding observations may have suggested. On the contrary: her poetry is created in a sophisticated way, both linguistically and "symbolically" (this will be mentioned later), and includes sections that are frankly experimental and manipulated. Her "virginity" is on another level; not the level of writing poetry, but the level of her engagement with such an act. In the act of writing poetry, she sees herself with perfect clarity and imposes a harsh discipline, resulting in a clear, critical distance from her poems and books. However, in relation to her poetic engagement *in toto* and her "poetic-Self," she has no objective distance. She accepts herself as a poet without taking issue, and sees no problem in that. For her, being a poet means a kind of "being-so" rather than "being-here-now" (*Sosein*, not *Dasein*). In sum: she took a step back from the poem and not from poetry. This second step is what problematises both Flexor and Guimarães Rosa. And from one's own perspective, this second step reveals the groundless abyss of nothingness. Why did Dora not take this step? This question, which does not trouble Dora is nonetheless one's decisive question relative to life as a whole and is the foundation for one's heated contact with Dora.

§ The question theoretically allows two answers.
One is that Dora did not take the second step
back because she dreads doing so (*und der Mensch
versuche die Götter nicht* – Let no Man tempt the Gods
– Schiller). The other answer is that she did not
take this step because she bumps into Something
whenever she tries (against David's shield – *Maguen*).
The third option, which implies that Dora does
not know how to take this step, is excluded. Dora
is an extremely lucid and highly sensitive spirit and
perfectly capable to surpass herself in the suggested
direction (she is not "primitive," in the sense of
being incapable of reflective thought, speaking
once again from a Marxist perspective). Thus, both
possible answers ("fear and trembling" and "faith")
may not even be different for Dora. For those who
fall within the objective distance of the second step,
however, the difference is decisive because it is the
difference between "perdition" and "salvation,"
between being entirely open or entirely closed.
One's experience with Dora and her *oeuvre* teach
(and it is thrilling to witness) that this difference
is only a problem for those who observe it from
an annihilating distance. At this point, however,
the methodological problem mentioned at the
beginning of this chapter reveals the extent of its
power: to establish a distinction of this sort would
be the basic criterion for judging Dora's poetry,
which is impossible for one who shares concrete
experience with her. In other words: concrete
experience, so enriching for the comprehension
of both Flexor and Guimarães Rosa's *oeuvres*, casts

a concealing shadow on one's comprehension of Dora's *oeuvre*. One must admit this fact without being able to explain it.

§ Nevertheless, there is no doubt that in order to be "faithful" and address ethico-religious concerns, the categories through which one judges an *oeuvre* must be more than aesthetic ones. This is true because these dimensions are intrinsic to Dora's poetry; they do not encase it, as with Guimarães Rosa. Rosean prose sits within a religious context; Dora's poetry is a religious articulation. Unfortunately, this is not the appropriate place for an analysis of such poetry – mostly for technical reasons. And Dora's poetry does not allow for generalised judgement, which is highly banal; it demands a patient analysis of each poem, each line, and each word. Some texts are meaningful only when read closely, and Dora's are a perfect example. To read her work is to dive into a universe where literally everything must be discovered. So it is useless, trying to draw generalised maps of this universe, since they would look like maps of the Americas from the end of the 15th-century. The only general comment that could be meaningfully stated about this universe is that it exerts the fascination of the unknown.

§ Leaving aside the problem of "intuition" Dora's *oeuvre* so virulently proposes – and knowing that "intuition" implies "vocation," therefore, "obedience" in the same sense as "*Chema Israel* = listen and obey, Israel" – and so, leaving aside what is essential to her *oeuvre*, several aspects can still be discussed. Even if Dora sees herself as an "instrument," and even if one feels perplexed, facing such an admission, a wide field of discussion with her still remains. And among the affectively discussed problems, the "symbol" occupies a prominent place, and may suffice to depict the climate of our dialogues and how they enriched and continue to enrich one's own thought and life. This is because everything considered with Dora points towards the realms of religiosity.

§ The problem of the symbol has always occupied a central position in one's own thought. If one's early interest focused on the philosophy of language, this was because one grasped and experienced language as a system of symbols. Later this interest widened and encompassed the field of communication, because the essence of communication and "mediation" is grasped and experienced as a process of symbolisation, as "*Sinngebung* = to give meaning." The problem of the symbol may be formulated in several ways. For example: the symbol is a phenomenon that represents another phenomenon, which is its meaning. A collection of symbols is therefore a universe that represents another universe. And this exactly describes the relationship between spirit and concrete reality. Another example: the symbol dialectically substitutes its meaning because it simultaneously presents and conceals it. That is what is meant when one says the symbol "represents." This dialectic of symbolic mediation is the fundamental problem of knowledge. Last example: the symbol is meaningful because it represents *another* phenomenon. Non-symbolic or non-representational phenomena are meaningless (for example: the universe of concrete things). And the symbols that have lost contact with the phenomenon they *should* represent (empty symbols) are equally meaningless (for example: pure "categorical" speculation). Therefore, to symbolise is to give the world meaning.

§ In a certain way, "symbol" is for us what "*logos*" was for Heidegger. However, one's method, imposed by the contemplation of the symbol, is the exact opposite of Heidegger's. In one's view, "to decodify" means to allow meaning to emerge through the symbol (in other words: to allow meaning to speak and thus reach the *thing-in-itself*, in the Husserlian sense), and not, as Heidegger would see it, to manipulate the symbol in order to force meaning to emerge. From this perspective, the theory of communication appears to promise (as a radical kind of decodification) a Husserlian path towards a theory of the thing because it eliminates Heideggerian anthropocentrism (Existentialism). In sum: one views the "symbol" as mediation between concrete subject and object, and "to decodify," means to de-alienate the subject. That is why one has always envisioned a synthesis of phenomenology, formal logic, and Marxism as the philosophical method of the future.

Vilém Flusser

§ For Dora, the symbol is an equally central problem, but it is not located primarily between the subject and the thing, but mediates instead between the subject and the transcendent. For her, the symbol's ultimate meaning is not a thing within the dimension of life, but something that lies beyond that dimension. Therefore, for Dora, the symbol is a vector pointing in the opposite direction of one's own vector. For her, the symbol is synonymous with *logos*, although not as in symbolic logic or Heidegger, but as in the *Stoa* and Christianity. For Dora, Christ as the *logos* is not only the ultimate symbol (mediation *par excellence*), but also the key symbol, which allows for radical decodification; the unlocking of every meaning. This vision, which is different from one's own, can be explained by our opposing views of the symbol's genesis: in one's view, the process of symbol generation is a human opus (conventional or not) enacted in order to overcome our fundamental human alienation; for Dora, symbol generation is a trans-human opus (revelation) enacted in order to overcome our fundamental human alienation (original sin). In other words, one sees the symbol as a human attempt to "endow meaning" upon an absurd world, and decodification as the rediscovery of the absurd. For Dora, the symbol is a channel through which all meaning is revealed, and decodification is the unveiling of profound meaning. At this point, the dichotomy that tears apart Western culture and our *being-in-the-world* becomes apparent: it is the dichotomy between Greeks and Jews. From the

Greek perspective, human alienation means the loss of immediate contact with the *topos uranos*, which is overcome through *logos* in the form of *Soter*. From the Jewish perspective, human alienation means the loss of immediate contact with the concrete world of things, which can be overcome by tearing the *logos*. For the Greeks salvation lies in the medium (in the *logos*), and for the Jews salvation lies in what is immediate (in the Sabbath as the overcoming of the *logos*). This is because, for the Greeks alienation is an "error" (*doxa*), while for the Jews alienation is a "sin" (*chata*), and logic means perdition, not salvation.

§ Obviously, none of us Westerners can escape such a dichotomy – not only because we harbour within us both views of alienation, but also because both views are constantly being integrated. We can be neither Greek (Vicente's mistake) nor Jewish (Zionism's mistake), because we can no longer distinguish between the two. They are fused within us in multiple ways – for example, in Christianity, science, and Marxism. There were moments in our history when the dichotomy seemed reestablished, for example, during the Renaissance and Reformation. But later we could see how much the Renaissance, which was apparently Greek, was actually Jewish, and how much the Reformation, which was apparently Jewish, was actually Greek. The most recent evidence of this is Husserl, who aspired to a Greek objective (*mathesis universalis*) while employing a Jewish method (*epoché* = Shabbat). One of the most productive influences Dora exerted on us was to expand this dichotomy at the level of both symbol and meaning.

§ For us, Dora's fundamental message is that the symbol is ambivalent, and that it can be seen as a vector toward the concrete thing and the transcendent (and therefore the concrete thing and the transcendent can be mistaken for one another). Hence, Dora curiously evokes medieval thought, kabbalah, alchemy, and Raymond Llull, to mention a few modes of thinking. It is not by chance but perfectly organic to her *forma mentis* that one of her series of poems (perhaps the most perfect one) is titled *Tapestries*. The symbolism of medieval tapestries (for example, those of Peaune and Angers, which one saw recently), with their perfectly logical structure, profoundly diaphanous beauty, apparent naivety, and elaborate sophistication, is a good entry into Dora's universe. For her, to write poetry is to weave de-alienating symbols that mediate between us and reality, which is trans-human. Writing poetry for her means to dive into prayer, and stepping back from poetry cannot be done: it would mean stepping backwards into the Other, in every sense. Accompanying her trajectory towards a borderline state *in fieri* has been a priceless privilege, an experience that has impacted one's entire life.

§ However, in order to situate our dialogue, one has to mention one other subject: Rilke. This will reveal the "formal" fecundity of our mutual sincerity. For Dora, Rilke is above all the creator of the *Duino Elegies*, which she translated superbly to Portuguese. From one's perspective, Rilke – despite being a current always flowing towards the *Elegies* and the *Sonnets* – is more present in some of the shorter poems like *The Panther, The Swan, The Prophet*, and *Der Tod is Gross*, because his essence is revealed here. This difference of opinion (which seems subaltern) is meaningful and needs to be elaborated upon. In one's opinion, Rilke's problem is as follows: how can one navigate the narrow path between kitsch and unbearable beauty and reach the outer limits of beauty? Rilke resolves this problem repeatedly in a way that is exceptionally surprising. For example, he rhymes *Munds* and *uns* in *Der Tod ist Gross*; he uses the word *geruht* in *The Swan*; he rhymes *verlassen* and *kassen* in *Die Könige der Welt sind alt*; and he uses the plural *"ihre bleichen Töchter"* and *"kranke Kronen"* in the same poem. Only after one has experienced this in the flesh in the *Elegies* can one grasp why Beauty – which is nothing but terror commencing – disdains to annihilate us. Kitsch as the horizon of Beauty (therefore, of *"man"* as the horizon of *"es"*) is, from one's perspective, Rilke's problem. That is why one sees Rilke as the link between Nietzsche and Heidegger, endowing an aesthetic dimension to the Nietzschean problem of the herd and the Heideggerian *Gerede* – small talk. Rilke is a forward-looking revolutionary because he reveals the terrible power of kitsch as the horizon of Beauty in the culture of the future. From this perspective, *Die*

Könige der Welt sind alt is the definitive poem and no analysis of "developmentalism" and mass culture can ignore it – both from the standpoint of content and form. Rilke essentially shows that the problem of kitsch is not an aesthetic issue, but a religious one. The word for this is "Orphic."

§ But this is not Dora's Rilke. Although she also feels the terrible danger of kitsch that Rilke represents and motions towards, and although she diligently struggles with that threat in her own practice, this is not what she finds moving in Rilke. Characteristically, in her translation of the *Elegies*, Rilke's kitsch aspects disappear completely. For example, *"Ein jeder Engel ist schrecklich"* becomes "every angel is terrifying" [*todo anjo é terrível*]. And, perhaps inevitably, *Dreizack* becomes "trident." By the way, one must say that the fundamental problem of translation only became clear for us after one's dialogue with Dora – maybe because the crystalline integrity of Dora's Portuguese makes her not only immune, but insensitive to any inherent kitsch. Note her superb use of internal alliteration, which is perfect and consistent, but dangerous when adopted by others (which does not mean that, when reading her poems, Dora did not find, together with us, certain dubious passages to be eliminated – proof of an incredible shared linguistic sensibility). For Dora, Rilke's problem is his ability to transform "ordinary" language (as meant by modern logic) into a transparent vehicle for transcendent meaning. For example, Rilke's use of the words *gelassen*, *brauchen*, or *Erde*, and the expression "*zu gut*" in the context "*zu gut unterscheiden.*" And his use of the word "*Doppelbereich*" and the plural "*Die Liebenden*" applied in the second person. For her, this is real poetry because it "breathes life" into worn out and dead words. Through her reading, Dora showed us a dimension of Rilke's work that one had only felt obscurely. She not only linked Rilke to Nietzsche but also to Goethe of the "*Fuellest wieder,*" thereby pointing out the subterranean connection between Rilke and Slavic poetry evident, not only for Prague writers (Jean Neruda and even Karel Mácha) but also, surprisingly, to Mayakovski. In this way, Rilke became organically connected to his contemporaries, the Russian formalists. Dora's reading of Rilke proves how those who consider him a "minor and decadent poet" – which is to say the majority of German critics today – are mistaken. Because of her experience and translation of the work, Dora penetrates Rilke better than the German critics – which is proof, if it were even needed, of the disastrously kitsch effect Nazism had upon Germany. Borrowing Rilke's words, Germany was where the "*kranken Kronen*" were handed over to "*Gewalt*" by the "*bleichen Töchter*" (the sickly crowns were handed over to violence by the pale daughters). That which died on the margins of the Isar and the Moldova rivers may rise again in Brazil, with a renewed spirit, thanks to artists such as Dora. If there is still any hope of a true "Brazilian project," Dora is the one who embodies it – and not the Trans-Amazonian project. This is an imbalanced struggle: between the translation of Rilke to Portuguese and the translation of technological progress to the Brazilian jungle. Kitsch will triumph and Dora cannot fight against Mogi das Cruzes. Whatever represents Brazil's real future must take refuge in Itatiaia, or in para-monastic circles, reading Meister Eckehart and decodifying symbols from a transcendent tradition. There is something incredibly beautiful and good being suffocated here (or "framed"), and one's role in this process is to serve as a witness to European plagues. A dark despair fills one's heart, having to reexperience this.

§ The Dialogue with Dora exists as the encounter between two beings, amidst a rising tide of kitsch, efficiency, and grandiloquence, who both feel the pulsation of beauty as religious *pathos*. If not for Dora, one would not have overcome the contradiction between Goodness and Beauty. Thanks to her, one reconquered *Kalokagathia*. However, and partly due to her, one despaired regarding the question of engagement, because one discovered that "alienation" is an ambivalent term. To engage in the world meant alienation from that which, through the mediation of symbols, gives life meaning. Unable to let go of this ambivalence, one had to disengage from the world and remain "suspended," waiting for Something. However, could not "suspension" mean, "They also serve who merely stand and wait"? Perhaps this question lies at the core of Dora's Being.

José Bueno

§ To theorise about the decadence of the social order is one thing; to experience it via an intimate and prolonged dialogue is another. This may be the complement of uprootedness. And perhaps there is no greater existential affinity between José Bueno and us. As a noble member of the decadent landowning class, with encyclopaedic culture, refined taste, sophisticated rules of rectitude, ethical and aesthetic behaviour, and a jaded, de-ideologised view of contemporary culture, José is perhaps what one would have become if the Nazis had not intervened in Prague's creeping decadence. In order to grasp this affinity, a parallel can be drawn: being uprooted means being expelled from one's reality, and belonging to a decadent order means witnessing the reality of one's immediate circumstance crumbling. José lives in a "Brazil" where he cannot recognise the Brazil that grounds him, or his own "Brazil" as the foundation of something new. He is rootless in his own land, because his class was displaced from the top of the social order by the immigrant *petit bourgeoisie*, which resulted in the ideological subversion of society. This is also because of the revolutionary modification of all of reality's structures, from the material (cultural things), to the immaterial (values, models, and aims). None of what structures José's *being-in-the-world* corresponds with society's structures. He is a stranger in the land his forbearers spent centuries shaping, while those who have recently

Vilém Flusser

arrived have become natives. And being a stranger in contemporary culture is not the only thing those of us over forty years old have in common. We are strangers in contemporary culture, but we are parents of the natives. We are strangers in a Camusian sense: José is a Martian in Brazil. His roots have stayed intact, but the earth to which they clung has disappeared; now the roots are suspended in nothingness. This is a complementary situation to one in which the roots were amputated – hence, our affinity.

§ Obviously, this constant situation, common to both of us, of being face-to-face with the void, to Nothingness and the Death of God, becomes articulated through several layers of experience and through our "explication of the world." But it becomes important through the attempt to grasp our dialogues and to highlight the specificity of the Brazilian situation as embodied by José. It is seemingly this: the immigrant *petit bourgeoisie* who currently holds and contests the power of decision in Brazil (as far as it is possible in a dependent country) is, like *petit bourgeoisie* everywhere: the victim of several ideologies that originated in the 19th-century on both the political right and left. In other words, it seeks to create either a technocratic society (the right) or a socialist one (the left). However, the dethroned class, which is almost feudal, having lost any ideology a long time ago (at least its most lucid representatives), is therefore far more politically conscious than the current class that dominates.

The decadent class is more "up to date" and open
to the present than this ascending, triumphal class.
Maybe this is nothing but one of the aspects of
the famous gap in development in underdeveloped
countries. Even so, it is an aspect of the current
Brazilian situation's tragedy. Althusser provides the
tools for analysis of this situation in his discussion
of the process through which Hegel's dialectics
turned into Marx's. Althusser's discussion shall
therefore be applied here to a discussion of the
Brazilian reality.

§ According to Althusser, the "inversion"
of Hegel as executed by Marx does not mean
simply a thematic inversion, in that Marx saw
as "immediate reality" what Hegel saw as "the
negation of reality." This inversion between the
roles of "matter" and "idea" would not have had
revolutionary consequences because it would have
left the dialectic structure intact. On the contrary,
Marx operated a revolution on the dialectic
structure itself in the following manner: for Hegel,
"becoming" is a logical process in which every
position necessarily implies its negation, and this
negation is necessarily overcome by a qualitative
leap. This is because *idea* for Hegel – pure logic – is
reality's infrastructure. For Marx, however, reality's
structure is matter in motion. Therefore, pure logic
cannot be the structure of "becoming." History
cannot be logical, but it is made so by the human
spirit. This means that the process of becoming is
not a simple Hegelian triad but extremely complex

and should be analysed at every step of the way. A simple contradiction is not sufficient to evoke a revolutionary leap. Every fundamental contradiction creates additional internal and external conditions, on multiple levels. And every level, together with its inherent contradictions, tends to become autonomous. An objective revolutionary situation only becomes real when every contradiction within a given situation becomes explosive, or when none of the levels can hold themselves together. This implies that no level can be satisfactorily "explained" by another: for example, the religious situation could never be entirely explained by the economic or social contradiction, which serves as its infrastructure. The levels are not only autonomous, but there is constant feedback between them. In sum: reality is complex and Hegel's mystification, his "idealism," was the attempt to simplify it. That is what Marx meant when he said that history advances along its "worst side." Revolution occurs where the contradictions are at their worst: not in England but in Russia, not in the United States but in China and the developing countries.

§ What characterises the Brazilian situation is not so much the contradiction at the level of production and work, but the contradiction within that contradiction: between worker and peasant, landowner and bourgeoisie. What characterises the latter situation is the fact that some of the landowners are more politically conscious than the bourgeoisie. The truly revolutionary element in

Brazil is not the proletariat (or the peasantry) but the decadent landowner, because the contradictions there have reached an explosive intensity. And this revolutionary function may become decisive, because the landowners still represent a considerable force. This partly explains the Church's position, too – although this is obviously nothing more than an "explicatory model" and must be applied with great care. However, it has the advantage of being a less simplistic model than the "traditional left," which turned Stalinistically towards Hegel's dialectic. This model also allows us to grasp the cultural and religious dimensions by which José's contradiction is more evidently manifested.

§ José experiences the decadence of reality as the death of God. This death manifests itself on multiple levels. On the religious level, it becomes tolerant indifference towards any already established or emerging religion – but with a longing for his own, lost religion. On the epistemological level, it manifests as disillusionment with every form of knowledge and distanced and ironic interest in any form of scientific or technological progress. On the ethical level, it manifests as adherence to a meaningless and historically bankrupt set of values. On the aesthetic level, it manifests as a refined eclecticism and a sharp eye for identifying kitsch. On the level of politics, it manifests as disdain for any ideology and the adherence to any situation that is vaguely bothersome. On the level of praxis, it manifests as going-with-the-flow, near

automatic action, immobility, and the avoidance
of any decisions or change. On the level of lived
experience, it manifests as depression and boredom.
In sum: the death of God means the loss of all
meaning. However, José's lucid spirit, his quick
and bright intelligence, his polemic temperament,
his violent – although repressed – energy, and his
human warmth all drive him to connect with others
and counteract all of the above. Hence, this basic
contradiction is what may become revolutionary at
any time, just as it may never ignite, and ultimately
die frustrated.

§ Our dialogues were ambivalent for José. They may
have contributed to preventing fertile explosions,
for both José and society, precisely because they
served as an escape valve for built-up tension.
However, these dialogue were extremely fertile for
us, not only because they allowed contact with
such a rich and profound world, but also because
they represented true friendship: an encounter
with someone in whom one recognised oneself. If
one's decision to cut ties with reality became more
painful, thanks to José; the decision became more
imperative because of him. The Brazilian Gordian
knot had to be cut in the hopes of preserving the
link connecting us to José, which is much stronger
than other links. Only the future will reveal if this
hope is justified since, for us, God is not dead: He
is alive in the Other.

DIALOGUE III

Romy Fink

§ "To come to know someone" is a process that might better be described as "learning the other is unknowable." The more one penetrates the other, the more one gets lost in his abysses. However, this description obscures the essence of the process. In reality, the other opens himself up to us as much as one opens oneself up to him. The abyssal mystery of the other is revealed by mutual suction ("attraction"), which is the essence of dialogue among friends. This mystery has nothing to do with "the problem of Man." For the anthropologist, Man is a complex system and therefore a problem to be solved. For a friend, the other is not a problem: he is a mystery.

§ Our direct experience with "mysterious" people contradicts this general observation. If everyone is mysterious, these people must be a "mystery within a mystery," which does not allow a friend to dive deeply inside them. Second-degree mysteries occur in two ways: either the friend butts against the other's resistance or he penetrates deeper into a kind of fog. In the first case, the person is mysterious because he hides something: a "secret." In these cases, frankness may emerge between the two parties, which allows for "the secret to be revealed." Thus, the mystery disappears. In the second case, there is no secret. There is only the discovery that the further one penetrates the other, the more he retreats. The first case is "analysable" (which includes the Freudian sense). The second resists analysis and detective work: there is no secret. There is no key to such a person; they are essentially mysterious.

§ However, this may lead the reader to a different conclusion. The reader may believe there was an aura of mystery surrounding one's friend Romy Fink when, in truth, it was just the opposite. Romy was a typical bourgeois with feet firmly planted on that soil the bourgeoisie believes to be reality. Among one's friends, he was the one who perhaps least doubted this reality. His mystery can be better grasped through a simple enumeration of facts — a method appropriate to his temperament.

§ Romy was an English Jew who showed up in São Paulo in the 1950s, a time when it was unusual for English Jews to emigrate. Some said he came as a lawyer for a textiles company from Liverpool, and much later this turned out to be true: he had been a successful lawyer in London. However, as far as one knew, he never worked as a lawyer in São Paulo. He had a modest life, teaching English with his wife. Some of his students accidentally discovered Romy was somewhat of "an authority on Shakespeare." He had published well-known texts on *Macbeth* and *Hamlet*. Heeding his students' insistence, he began to write and publish on Shakespeare in the press.

Then it emerged that Romy had worked in theatre in London – and not only in theatre, but the ballet. For many years, Romy had been the director of the Monte Carlo Ballet and had written a "ballet theory" with a preface by S. Diaghilev. He had even worked with the English Opera and was one of the Queen's official musicians and considered an authority on the production of Verdi's work.[15]

15. Some of these claims are exaggerated and others can be easily verified as inaccurate. In the pre-internet age, however, such claims enhanced the mystery of the friend with an unknown past. Today that mystery can be extinguished by a simple internet search.

§ This was not the focus of his activity in São Paulo, however. By some random chance, it surfaced that Romy had written some books on Persian art and Japanese ceramics and art criticism on modern painting for the *Times Literary Supplement.* Some Brazilian critics convinced him to write about Brazilian painting, which led to him opening a gallery on Augusta Street. Within a few years, Romy's gallery became one of the major ones in Brazil, which turned Romy into a very rich man.

§ Others discovered, also by chance, that Romy was a renowned Talmudist, descendant of a famous rabbinic family in Germany – hence, the name "Romy." Small reading groups formed to read the *Talmud* with him. Unfortunately, one did not take part in these, due to a lack of personal training. Nonetheless, one did have Talmudic discussions with Romy, which will be touched upon later. Within this context, it also became known that Romy was also a connoisseur of Jewish mysticism: the Kabbalah and especially the Zohar. He once confessed, almost casually, that he had participated in esoteric experiences, and that these experiences were the reason he left England. However, everything about him still remains a mystery.

§ Independent of any of this, rumours emerged regarding his activities during the war. Some said his family dealt with diamond cutting and that Romy put this service at England's disposal, which elevated him to high positions. One never managed to obtain more information on the matter. Additionally, Romy kept some surprising company. Famous theatre and cinema actors stayed at his house whenever they came to São Paulo. A Confucian Chinese painter living in Campinas turned out to be a close friend. North American psychology professors consulted him. He was in touch with obscure aristocratic Bulgarian Rabbis and lawyers. And he mingled with the Brazilian high bourgeoisie (especially bankers), with whom he organised painting exhibitions all over Brazil. However, he only really felt at home on one's terrace.

§ The most important element in all of this was that Romy did not hide anything – and he had no reason to. He simply did not talk about it. Even so, one could not comprehend how he could fit so much into sixty years and why he had moved to São Paulo. Thus, this was the external side of Romy's mystery.

§ There was, however, a more interesting side: the internal, religious one. Romy was an orthodox Jew. One had obviously met others: Rabbis, a Russian salesman, and some "primitive" (from the Western perspective) residents of the Bom Retiro neighbourhood of São Paulo. But one never had contact with them. Jewish religiosity has always seemed incomprehensible. One is "assimilated" and lives within Christianity, and whenever an assimilated Jew loses faith, it is actually the Christian faith he or she loses. One must admit that, from one's perspective, Jewish religiosity is far stranger than *macumba*. Romy therefore opened up for us the doorway to the mystery of Judaism.

§ Of the many experiences offered by Romy, one shall highlight two: ritual and humble deference to the Other. Of course, nothing is really comprehensible outside the concrete context of Romy's life. One hopes, however, that in the short sketch that follows some portion of this context will shine through for the reader.

§ Every Saturday afternoon, one gathered all of our friends on one's terrace. The discussions carried on until late at night. Among the participants were some of the friends who have already been mentioned, some who will be mentioned and others who will not, as well as some of one's students. Romy always arrived first, having walked the five kilometres from his house. Once the Sabbath was over, his wife came to pick him up by car. He never ate the food one's wife prepared because it was not "kosher." Not driving the car on Saturdays and not eating *treife* were a ritual part in the terrace gatherings, which sanctified the Sabbath and opened the transcendent for him. Thus, Romy feted the Sacred.

§ One discussed this several times with Romy. But it was only by observation that one realised: he radiated happiness. One finally comprehended that the Jewish commandments and prohibitions were not limitations but openings into a holy and festive life (festive as opposed to Vicentine[16]). Therefore, Jewish ritual means this: formalism with an entry into the existentially true.

16. Saint Vincent de Paul.

§ Sabbath means this: to delve into the concrete meaning of life along with others in search of transcendence. And this is what matters; human society is the means not the end. The friends gathered not to come together but to discuss. That is why they are friends, despite their conflicting views. For Judaism, "politics" is not what it is for the Greeks. It does not mean searching for a perfect society, but a society that allows the Sabbath (the Messiah) to shine through.

§ This holy society ("theocratic") must be ordered according to absurd laws so that it can be sanctified: by Jewish rituals. Wherever the social rules are reasonable (efficient, functional etc.), society is profane. Jewish rituals are festive because they are absurd. And because they are festive, they endow meaning to life. They are the opposite of pagan rituals. They are anti-magic; they do not have an aim. To want to "explain" Jewish rituals (for example, ethically) means to fall into paganism. If understood well, they are "sacrifices," although not happy sacrifices. This is not the case of sacrificing something (Iphigenia) in order to gain something (the defeat of Troy). Thus, one came to understand Abraham and Isaac from a Jewish perspective, as well as Romy's anti-Zionism. Israel is a society and not a ritual, which is why it is meaningless, even though it allows a certain space for Jewish rituals. Life is either entirely a ritual and therefore holy, or it is profane. To attempt to inject rituals into daily life is a sin. Romy lived festively: he was Jewish.

§ One had never encountered this before. One did not identify with other orthodox Jews one had met. They were "exotic" and did not share one's culture. But Romy was an Englishman engaged with Brazil; he was a Westerner, like oneself. The same type of art, science, and philosophy united us. He was one's friend and he was Jewish nonetheless. There was a limit, however. One never managed to live the ritual like he did. One was constantly interpreting the ritual, as an *aete gratuit*, an absurd gesture. One did not manage to amputate one's Greek dimension, one's *"Theoria."* One did feel admiration for Judaism, long for it and feel envious of Romy. But one did not manage to live according to Judaism.

§ The second aspect of Judaism that Romy showed us was religious deference to the Other. When one first met him, one felt repulsion for his exaggerated courtesy. He paid the greatest compliments, which one interpreted as being insincere. Much later, one sensed a profound humility behind this insincerity, which one did not comprehend. One hated it because it seemed like the "humility of the ghetto." Then one suddenly understood it, after Romy explained his behaviour in terms of the *Talmud*. He explained it not in order to justify himself or convince us, but because "such is life." Apropos, this lack of missionary zeal is a terrible thing in Judaism. He explained that, for the *Talmud*, there is only one irredeemable sin: to offend the Other. Everything else can be amended, and only an amends can redeem it. But to offend someone is irredeemable, since it hurts the Other's essence (the "soul"), which can never heal, because the Other's essence is Him (blessed be thy Name), and one can only concretely experience Him through the Other's essence. That is why there is only one God, but with as many versions as there are people and others (even though we do not recognise these *others* as people).

§ If one offends the Other, one offends Him, and if one serves the Other, one serves Him, and this is the only valid form of Divine service. Other types of service are entirely pagan. If one believes in God, then how one performs it is meaningless (this is one's own type of gymnastics). One can only find

salvation through the Divine act of serving the
Other. The highest Jewish commandment "Love thy
God above all else!" is synonymous with "Love thy
neighbour." The rest is hypocrisy.

§ Judaism is thus a political praxis in a
"transcendent" sense. Romy lived this way. One
found it existentially impossible to live in this
manner. Existentially, one is not Jewish. From one's
perspective, "to offend the Other" only means to
offend the mask, the "person," and not what lies
behind it. One does not believe that this human
essence can be offended. That is why one is never
offended. One is essentially Greek. One cannot
follow Romy. However, one's conscience aches for
not being able to follow him. One knows that the
only way to serve Him is through engagement. One
knows that the rest is hypocrisy. One knows that
one is responsible, and that one offends the Other
by not acting. And one knows, *hic et nunc*, that this
is Hell: for example, to not see Him in Chile. And
one also knows that this is why Judaism is not
missionary: it does not aim to save others, but to
sacrifice itself for them. However, this knowledge
does not help one.

§ One's religious experience holds us back. One
does not experience Him in the Other, but in
one's solitude before the wholly different; in one's
intimate moment; asocially. From one's perspective,
the religious experience in politics means
"superficiality." This is one's own type of hypocrisy.

Groundless

In this sense, one is Christian. One knows only too well that there is no fundamental difference between Judaism and Christianity. One knows that Judaism allows for an intimate experience of God and that Christianity also allows for a politico-religious form of engagement. However, there is a different accent between these two forms of religiosity, and the older one gets, the more this seems to be the real distinction – not the figure of "Christ." This belief is the consequence of one's religious isolation. Despite having a heavy conscience, one cannot *engage* in the Jewish sense of the term. This is why one abandoned Brazil: in order to seek interiority. One existentially chose Dora over Romy, although out of bad conscience (therefore, in bad faith), which according to the *Talmud*, and as Romy explained, is an irredeemable sin.

§ Romy died suddenly in New York in 1972. He died an entirely different death than the others described in this book. He died at approximately the same age as Vicente, Flexor, and Guimarães Rosa: the "best age." However, death turned Vicente into an amputated torso and, for Flexor, death was the enemy against which he painted. For Guimarães Rosa, it was destiny. For Romy, though, death was an integral, "normal," part of life. He died complete. His life was always whole, at any given moment, because it was a festive life. Death can do nothing to such a life. Rilke says: "let each one have an appropriate death." The other three died inappropriate deaths. They should not have died.

Romy died an appropriate death. God willing we shall all die how Romy did. But in order to die like this, we must live as Romy did.

Miguel Reale

§ The methodological problem of this book now emerges from a new angle. To be clear, all of one's partners in dialogue have been described, until now, as they presented themselves to us and not "objectively." One intends to follow in the same pattern with Reale. However, in the present case, the projected image will probably not coincide with any aspect of his "public" image. The explanation for this is that, among one's friends, Reale is the only "politician," in the strictest sense. Politicians are masks (*"personae"*) and actors (*"drontes"* [δρώντες]). The following description will not show Reale's person; it will show his personality, but it will not be an unmasking. For a real politician, the person is at least as authentic as the personality. Unmasking a politician is a pointless task, and biographies of Napoleon Bonaparte written by his coachman are cheap literature. One's dialogues with Reale do not unmask him, but reinforce the guise he adopted, both theoretically and existentially. His mask remains suspended during our dialogues, though, because the personality he adopts is captivating. In order to avoid any misunderstandings, one needs to point out that the personality is our friend, not the person *per se.*

Groundless

§ One shall present the "political persona" first, before attempting to depict the personality. Reale held the Philosophy of Law Chair at the University of São Paulo. He was the university's Rector several times, held the position of State Secretary, and of Chief Commissioner heading the reorganisation of the Brazilian Penal Code. He was a right wing politician and the ideologue for the military *coup d'état* of 1964. Reale authored basic works of philosophy, was the President and *spiritus rector* of the Brazilian Institute of Philosophy, and was more or less the official representative of Brazilian philosophy. That is how he is seen at large.

§ However, our dialogues, which spanned decades, were not as intense as the ones already described. There was a certain distance between us, although a sincere friendship united us. The dialogues with Reale were different in that they did not take place on one's terrace and Reale did not attend the weekend gatherings with friends. Our dialogues took place in his library, one of the richest in São Paulo. Reale was, unfortunately almost always surrounded by a Greek chorus of admirers, careerists, and opportunists who functioned as a *baso continuum* to our exchanges: a plague that afflicts the "powerful." And our dialogues almost always had a pretext: the Institute, the University, or a congress. This weakened their intensity. However, we generally managed to get through the pretexts quickly and to advance towards our mutual points of interest: "historicity, responsibility, and freedom." Let it be said that of all of Reale's works, the one that moves us the most is *Pluralism and Freedom.*[17]

17. Reale, M. *Pluralismo e Liberdade.* Edição Saraiva. São Paulo, 1963.

§ We approached these points not only from different angles but also from different cultural backgrounds. The reader knows one's origins. Reale is the son of Italian immigrants. Here two cultures met: the decadent descendant of the high bourgeoisie and the universal intellectual who had just broken out of the *petit bourgeoisie* bubble. Remnants of this bubble still clung to him, though: figurines on the mantelpiece, a "healthy" morale, and a hungry ambition. They contrasted with his high cultural level but enhanced him. These culturally strange elements shocked us as much as a few of one's own cultural elements must have shocked him. However, one quickly forgot them when confronted with his noble attitude and the speed and depth of his analyses. The cultural differences were not the only thing that set us apart; there were also differences in how we approached three specific problems.

§ From one's perspective, the problem of historicity, responsibility, and freedom are the ultimate problems. They are the aim of every discourse because they can only be answered through the praxis of concrete living. One cannot see how to approach these problems except through Marxism. However, this path must be examined and challenged before dealing with these problems.

In sum: one sees these problems as existential; as tasks. For Reale, they are the starting points for every possible discourse. First he asks, "Where am I?" And until he has clearly answered this question, every discourse is meaningless. For example, Marxism is only one among the discourses that result from these problems, and not a path from which to gain access to these problems. This view is due to the fact that one comes from a situation where history lost its meaning and responsibility means to accept the absurd; where freedom is impossible, and hence the question of human dignity. Reale comes from a society that shelters him. But in doing so, it imposes itself upon him as a problem.

§ Reale's answer to this problem can be exposed in two ways. Either theoretically, by taking our dialogues and his writings as a foundation; or concretely, from what is called in Brazil "the Brazilian reality." One chooses the second option. As for the first option, one has already published several essays on the matter in the European press.

§ The problem of historicity takes a different form in Brazil from that in Europe. If we define "history" as the sum of all deeds (*res gestae*), but not all suffering, then there is no Brazilian history. Brazil is an object and not a subject of Western history. In Brazil, "historicity" means the process of becoming aware of this fact. This is one's initial step towards ending this process and becoming a subject. In Europe, "historicity" means to accept oneself as the active product of one's own culture. However, this does not mean that Brazil is a "colony" in the strict sense. In a colonial situation "historicity" means to become the object of a foreign culture. Thus, in Brazil, this means to become the patient object of one's own culture. In the process of becoming aware of this historicity, Brazil does not become a colony, but a kind of exile from Western culture.

§ The problem of responsibility also takes a different form in Brazil from that in Europe. As the object of someone else's decision, one becomes irresponsible, which is the climate of every reified situation. Every discussion within this situation tends towards irresponsible small talk and only serves to ideologically obscure the situation. The problem one faces, therefore, is to discover where real responsibility is found, and once found, to maximise it within its narrow limits. By widening the field of authentic responsibility, one shall have taken a decisive step towards entering Brazil into history. In Europe, the opposite is true. European society is burdened with excessive responsibility. Europe has to limit its field of competence in order to make its historical burden bearable. In sum: in Brazil one has to take on greater responsibility in order to enter history. In Europe, one has to limit one's responsibility in order to exit history with dignity.

§ Finally, the problem of freedom is entirely different in Brazil from Europe. Structurally, Brazil is not a free society (despite the feeling of existential freedom, which Europe denies). Brazil is a society that is subject to foreign manipulation. This lack of freedom manifests itself in every arena, from the economic to the cultural, except on the political level, where a phantom of "independence" – or freedom – hovers. However, this political freedom has always been a cover for the lack of freedom (both individual and collective), which the so-called "democratic" periods illustrate dramatically. The problem of freedom in Brazil lies in the question of how to open up the field for freedom within an objectively given situation of reification. That is why a real revolution has never been possible in Brazil. In Europe, "the mother of revolutions," freedom is a question of the relation between the individual and society.

§ For Reale, these are the coordinates of the problem. And since Reale is one of the few people who can clearly see the coordinates, this imposes a task upon him: to awaken historical consciousness, provoke a sense of responsibility, and create the conditions for real freedom. All of his theoretical and practical engagement boils down to this: to contribute to opening up the field of freedom for the Brazilian individual and society. His philosophy work aims to be a foundation for his engagement, and his work as a professor, rector, and politician attempt to translate these foundations into praxis.

Reale is one of the few Brazilians dedicated in both body and soul to the ideal of freedom.

§ However, this kind of dedication has paradoxical consequences. One shall give three examples. Reale sees himself, so to speak, as forced to extract Brazil from its own context. He knows perfectly well that the power of the bourgeoisie is under threat all over the world. But he feels forced to place his trust in the Brazilian bourgeoisie because they are the only group capable of historical consciousness in Brazil right now. In his view, the proletariat is incapable of this consciousness – and the peasantry even less. One fears that Reale trusts the bourgeoisie too much, due to his own bourgeois prejudices. However, his analysis is undoubtedly correct, there could not be any spontaneous workers' movement in Brazil right now,[18] and therefore, a revolution cannot happen. This is all pure demagogy, but one cannot be certain if Reale is aware of this terrible fact. And one is not sure whether, when consigning his hope in the Brazilian bourgeoisie, if he is aware that it is dependent on the international bourgeoisie, and that, if one falls, the other follows it.

§ The second paradoxical consequence is that the reification of Brazilian society has economic roots because it is from the economic perspective that Brazil serves as an object to others. Hence, it is irrational to sever this situation overnight: this would only result in a shift from one centre

18. This was written in 1973, seven years before the founding of the Brazilian workers' party (PT).

of decision to another, probably more nefarious one. The only reasonable possibility is to develop the economy, so that in the future it may become capable of a meaningful self-liberating movement. This development of the economy demands technocracy (or is at least made possible through it). However, technocracy is structurally fascist because it tends to reduce politics and culture. Reale opts for technocracy as a lesser evil. Thus, he denies himself, which is an important aspect of his tragedy, because he is a man of politics and culture. Reale knows with absolute clarity that freedom is a political and cultural question. Nevertheless, he opts against it. This is a tragedy in the precise sense of the term.

§ The third paradoxical consequence one shall mention is this: Reale feels forced to tolerate the dominant and alienating ideologies, as well as support them with his culture. One can understand the strategy behind this. Admittedly, these ideologies are alienating, but they are instruments to overcome an intolerable situation. One believes Reale intends to use these ideologies as tools. He is above them. However, in the end, he is the one who ends up being used. Perhaps he even accepts this tragic fact as a kind of sacrifice of the intellect.

§ Reale is an extremely rare thing: a man with pure motives, fundamental honesty, and integrity. He has always used the power at his disposal to support and broaden the freedom and dignity of both individuals and society. It is important to note this for posterity. He is rare in the sense that he is one of the few individuals able to see the current situation clearly, without prejudice. One may explain his situation like this: he proposes to sacrifice himself for society. From the outside, only the mask is visible: the establishment's tool. Behind it, one sees the personality that wears the mask: the freedom fighter.

§ One always found this vision extremely moving. And from one's own perspective, it is the consequence of a completely mistaken attitude, because one sees the role of the intellectual in society through a different prism. One agrees with Reale that his role is to awaken social consciousness. But one disagrees that, in order to do this, he must opt for one of the existing ideologies. One must fight against all of them. Within the Brazilian context, this means the intellectual must reveal the situation as one sees it – and Reale does see it correctly. Given the fact that this is a tragic situation, the role of the intellectual is then equally tragic: negative critique. Otherwise, no matter which position one adopts in such a situation, it means to surrender to an impossible exit. In other words, this is the intellectual's choice as one sees it: to remain faithful to one's Self and become innocuous, or to surrender.

§ And yet, as one writes this, one is forced to pause. Which is the greater tragedy: Reale's or ours? Maybe Reale is authentically "political" and therefore an intellectual: politics becomes the art of possibility and the sacrifice of the intellect. As one could not have made this impossible decision, one excused oneself and forfeited one's own responsibility. One kept one's hands "pure." Or, in other words: one allowed one's burden to fall away. All the same, one could not have done it differently. Reale's example showed us that this was not the path one could have followed.

§ There are obviously fundamental differences between the two of us in relation to this problem. However, they do not touch the existential choice mentioned above. Rather, our differences are these: unlike Reale, one does not believe that to enter history is necessarily a good thing for society. Unlike him, one does not believe that Brazilian society could be freed, simply through the Liberation of "Brazil" (one is not even sure what this term means). One does not believe that the Brazilian problem could be faced (much less resolved) outside its context, which is, in many ways, revolutionary. One is convinced that the Western bourgeois world is in a deep crisis, and that it will not overcome its crisis (the Brazilian problem must be seen against this backdrop). And fundamentally, one believes that in this current situation (Brazilian and international) any type of engagement ends up benefiting the various established orders. However, none of this alters the existential nature of the problem: "how must

one act as an intellectual here and now?" Reale is
answering this question. One is unable to do so.
That is why, despite disagreeing with Reale, one
deeply admires him and respects his brave and
courageous existential decision.

Mira Schendel

§ The dialogue about to be described tracks the
curve of a fever. The oscillation of the curve is
a result of Mira's character and she controls the
course that unites us. Not that she manipulates us
as her instrument; on the contrary, she is extremely
open to other people. However, she has a degree
of intolerance and subconscious fanaticism that
make her treat as an object everyone with whom
she comes into contact. If her dialogue partner is
weak, that person runs the risk of being annihilated
(completely against her desire and will, since Mira
is a lonely soul in search of authentic company).
However, if her dialogue partner is capable of
resisting her (which one believes is our case), sparks
ignite. In this "electric" sense, one's contact with
Mira has been very fruitful, although it demanded
measures of patience, which one normally does
not have. One's patience was mobilised in Mira's
case for two unrelated reasons: one admires her as
an artist (possibly the greatest artist one has ever
had contact with), and Mira inspires unlimited
trust, thanks to her moral and intellectual integrity
(which is synonymous perhaps with friendship). In

short, despite the rollercoaster ride, we are always in constant friendship.

§ One shall attempt to reduce one's dialogue with Mira down to two primary points. These apply not just to Mira's work, but they are also the primary points around which contemporary visual art orbits: "transparency" and "meaning." One shall attempt to grasp these two themes in two different ways. The first will reflect upon the manner in which these arise in our dialogues. The second will reflect upon the way in which they manifest in Mira's oeuvre. There is feedback, however, between these two methods of observation. Our dialogues influenced her work and the works were also the subject of our dialogues. This feedback enriched our relationship: one is Mira's authentic critic and Mira is the authentic subject of one's thoughts and studies.

§ "Transparency" is a result of the human eye's ability to see through the surface of things. This ability is what distinguishes the human eye from other ways of seeing. The human gaze is not necessarily conditioned by the surfaces, and this is why humans do not live in an enclosed environment, but their gaze can penetrate surfaces (in a raw and disciplined way) and open up the dimension of depth, which transforms their world into a *Lebenswelt* (a world for human life). One spoke of two types of piercing methods: raw and disciplined. The raw gaze (for example, phenomenology, art, and mysticism) tears the surfaces and reveals the abysses behind things. The disciplined gaze (for example, scientific research) penetrates surfaces and discovers increasingly general, formal, and empty foundations. Therefore, the disciplined gaze is progressive; it becomes increasingly more formal and empty. Today, it begins to discover the same abysses that the raw gaze customarily revealed. Thus, the world we live in melts into nothingness. The world is becoming transparent – not in the sense that we can no longer see anything, but in the sense that now we see transparent structures, which allow us to see other transparent structures, around us in all directions, including inside. We are becoming transparent to ourselves. Every object begins to dissolve. As a result, no longer *exist*. "To exist" means *being* in an objective world, and where there is no object, there is no subject. This was the first point of focus.

§ "Meaning" is what symbols point to. Symbols are either consciously or unconsciously conventional things that represent other things. Whoever participates in the convention (and can "decodify" the symbols) discovers the things, which are the meanings, represented by the symbols. The meanings of symbols can also be other symbols, and so hierarchies emerge. One of the main problems of contemporary communication theory is the arrangement of every symbol within its place in the hierarchy. However, the main premise of this theory is that there are some things that are not symbols (the so-called "concrete things"). These concrete things are the ultimate meaning of every symbol, the ground upon which the whole hierarchy rests. To produce symbols under this premise means to give meaning to the world of concrete things. Every new symbol lands in the concrete world as if from a new angle, and therefore increases the amount of meaning in the world. This is the function of the so-called "spirit": to constantly propose new symbols and new codes in order to increase the amount of meaning in the world. This was the second point of focus.

§ So if the world is becoming increasingly transparent, this is because it is losing its concreteness. In such a world, everything becomes a symbol. Everything can therefore signify anything else, and this is a way of saying that there are no decisive meanings in this world. In a final analysis, "transparency" is the potential to see meaning in everything, and "meaning" is the potential to transform everything into a transparent thing. In such a situation, it does not matter that "spirit" becomes meaningless. Furthermore, any engagement with art also becomes meaningless. Hence, these two focal points shaped our dialogues, which will be demonstrated by examining two of Mira's artworks.

§ A picture is suspended from the ceiling in the middle of a room. It is made up of two flat pieces of acrylic plastic that are approximately one metre and fifty centimetres long by one metre and fifty centimetres wide. Between the acrylic plates are several pieces of rice paper. Black marks have been drawn on the paper and onto the four surfaces of the acrylic plates (internal and external surfaces). The following marks stand out: printed and hand-drawn letters, numbers, and scribbles. The whole picture is almost perfectly transparent. The viewer can see the work from both sides, two texts that are different not only because they mirror one another, but because they invert each other's depth. Because the layout of the text is transparent, the viewer sees the room through the text, and as the plate shifts with the breeze, the viewer sees the text dynamically from his or her viewpoint. If the viewer attempts to read the text, she discovers messages laid out in several directions: horizontally, vertically, diagonally, and in the illusionistic depth of the image. Several kinds of messages emerge: words, images, and shapes. The words could be drawn from several languages, but the viewer will always feel that he discovered the words and not that Mira implanted them. Images are merely suggested, such as an army of "A"s advancing toward the viewer. The forms are geometric (for example, spirals), but they are never clearly outlined. No matter in which direction the viewer looks, she will always find some meaning. However, the text as a whole is completely meaningless. The work has incredible aesthetic power: it is fascinating, absorbing, and it dominates the room.

§ The other artwork is a sketchpad approximately thirty centimetres long by twenty centimetres wide and containing around forty pages (this is a description from memory, so one could be mistaken). It belongs to Mira's sketchpad series. In describing it, one weakens the sketchpad's essence by eliminating its progressive dimension: one can move from sketchpad to sketchpad. The sketchpad's pages are transparent and can be leafed through traditionally or flipped around the spine. They offer two texts: on the right, near the spine, and on the left. The theme for this sketchpad is the letter "b," which appears on most of the pages, loosely rendered or touching either the inner or outer circumference of a circle. Flipping through the pages, the letter "b" dances like magic lantern shadows or slides on a zoetrope. If we rotate the pages, we see a variety of texts consisting of the letter "b," according to the number and sequence of pages transparently overlaid. The important thing to note is that the "b" leaps from the third dimension to a curious fourth one in a way that is not clearly evident, forming almost surreptitiously a "d," "p," and "q." It is almost as if we could magically transform our left hand into our right one – then make the two overlap. This feels like a symptom of real art: simplicity, clarity, and mystery, existing as a task that absorbs one's interest.

§ The acrylic work was shown at the Venice Biennale and the sketchpad at the São Paulo Bienal. Mira gave us these artworks, which one keeps at home.

Vilém Flusser

One wrote about the first piece for the Brazilian press. Hence, one believes to have contributed towards the public understanding of Mira's work, and towards Mira's own self-understanding. She sent the translation of one's critique to Max Bense in Stuttgart. He "did not understand" it. Bense's lack of understanding is a symptom of the aesthetic crisis in art today.

§ Both works could be viewed from at least three perspectives: as experiments, as toys, and as new types of objects. One shall touch upon the "toy" and "object" perspectives and linger longer on the "experiment" angle.

§ As a toy, the sketchpad is a more developed version of the acrylic plate. Both artworks allow the viewer to invent their own texts and to enjoy the pleasure of creativity. However, the sketchpad is more ludic because it allows physical handling. Through her intelligence, sensitivity, and expert craftsmanship, Mira engages not only the gaze but also the sense of touch, and she invites viewers to play with her, in a literal sense. However, they are only toys to those who are on the same wavelength as Mira. One could say more about the ludic aspect of Mira's work, but one shall refrain from doing so here.

§ In my opinion, the acrylic plate as an object — although it was made earlier — is an evolution from the sketchpad. The primary characteristic of Mira's artworks, as objects, is that they are "transparent" – but in an opposite way from what we are accustomed to. Other objects seem to be opaque, but become transparent under the penetration of our gaze. Mira's objects impose themselves upon our gaze, setting up an inverted dynamic. They demand our gaze, in order to make them opaque. They force us into an inversion in relation to things, to a *"Kehre"* [Return], to cite Heidegger. These things must not be "explicated" (they are excessively clear); they must be condensed (we must "involve" ourselves with them). In this sense, they are "revolutionary" objects and point towards a possible future. However, one must also refrain from the impulse to write too much about the "thing" aspect of Mira's work.

§ As experiments, Mira's artworks have occupied one's thinking for a long time. They are attempts to transform ideas into conceivable objects. Mira seeks to translate the *concept* of transparency and the *concept* of meaning into an *image* of concept and an *image* of meaning. She attempts to invert the traditional relationship between imagination and discursive reason. This works as follows: (a) one sees something concrete in the course of everyday life. Then one attempts to transform it into an image in order to master it; (b) one seeks to transform the image at hand into a concept in order to manipulate one's concrete context. Historically speaking, phase (a) corresponds to the mythico-magical stage of culture and phase (b)

Vilém Flusser

to the epistemological-technical stage of culture. Mira's artworks belong to a posterior phase. Mira works in the following manner: (a) she finds a concept in everyday life and seeks to transform it into an image in order to comprehend it; (b) she seeks to transform the image into a concrete thing. Therefore, Mira's work performs a violently de-alienating function. One of the primary elements of our alienation is the unimaginable nature of our concepts. This alienation may be overcome through a new imaginative power, which Mira offers us.

§ This is extremely important because it implies a new type of *being-in-the-world*. Until now, we have been in the world, struggling against the concrete world. We objectify this world by mediating it through images. And we objectify the world of images by mediating it through concepts. Therefore, we are subjects of this world and simultaneously alienated from it. Today, as Mira and others' experiments show, we attempt to objectify the world of concept by mediating it through images, thus becoming subjects of our own concepts (their owners). We shall live, henceforth, not among concepts, but among images of concepts. This manner of *being-in-the-world* may be called "structural" because we shall live among structures. Or it may be called "post-historical" because we shall live among imaginatively synchronised processes. Mira represents one of the first advances towards this reformulation of the human concept.

§ It is a pity that Mira lives on the fringe of society. One sees it as one's duty to initiate her into the world. One hopes this essay will contribute to such an introduction. Thus, it will represent the continuation of one's dialogue with her.

Retrospective

§ With a retrospective, inverted gaze aimed at São Paulo, one will contemplate the scene on our terrace during the weekends. The terrace forms an organic link between a subtropical garden and a series of open rooms in the house, and it can be accessed only by traversing these rooms. The visitor, having passed through the gate, which is always open, and the front door, which is usually open, enters a foyer. In the foyer, which contrasts with the heat, pressure, and noise on the street, hang watercolours by Flexor. The sitting room is filled with artworks by the Brazilian avant-garde; Mira's acrylic plate dominates the room. A small library follows this, and then another room filled with paintings. The visitor then steps onto the terrace, generally unseen by those who live in the house. On the terrace, the visitor finds a group of friends engaged in passionate dialogue, either in a large circle or a number of smaller ones. Who are the friends and who is the visitor? One's retrospective glance falls upon a group of figures too large to be described here. Hence, one is forced unwillingly and with melancholy to let go of most of them for now. The ones described so far must function as representatives for all the others, as well as the foremost sectors of Brazilian culture. Together, with all their contradictions, hopes, disappointments, and activities, they represent a culture searching for an identity and which begins to lose hope of ever finding one.

§ In another sense, however, these figures are neither representative of Brazilian culture or of the terrace. They had something in common, though: the Brazilian youth. The majority of the people gathered on the terrace were my students, friends of my children, and friends of their friends. They formed the ground upon which the dialogic battles we fought resonated. They were the academic youth, the children of the bourgeoisie, between the ages of twenty and thirty years old. In hindsight, if one were to look for synchrony in the dynamic of the terrace, this would be its structure: for over twenty years, a variety of young people arrived like a series of tides, washing up on the shore of a more or less stable group of adults (artists, writers, scientists, and thinkers). The adult-nucleus did not change greatly over the years; it was only gnawed away by time and death. However, the tides of young people changed deeply, which gives this retrospective an outlook on "history" as a process that modifies Man.

§ There was a clear rupture to this process: the Coup of 1964. However, the Coup had a delayed effect upon the young. More than three years passed before the effects of the Coup altered the situation for the young. By 1968, however, the Brazilian situation had been fundamentally transformed. One shall attempt to describe the young both before and after '68, as well as the process of change.

§ What is surprising is that, before the Coup of 1964, the youth were more alienated from reality than the ones afterwards. Nineteen-sixty-four had the opposite effect on the young elite than it did on the masses. For academic youth, it meant a catastrophe that destroyed their illusions. For the masses, it meant the beginning of a thickening of scientifically manipulated ideologies. For young people, the catastrophe was followed by a period of merciless repression and resulted in a feeling, on the one hand, of powerlessness, and on the other, a desire to become part of the apparatus. Before one describes the process, however, one must issue a word of warning. The young people who gathered at our terrace were not, statistically speaking, the best representation of academic youth as a whole. They came from all the universities, including the "scientific" ones and the polytechnic ones. But they were primarily interested in the "humanities;" their presence on the terrace was evidence of this. Therefore, they suffered the impact more keenly than the majority of students.

§ Before 1964, young people lived under the illusion that Brazil was the soil upon which a new culture and a new way of life would be born. They saw themselves as responsible for this foundation. This bestowed upon them a particular attitude: they were extremely curious, willing to learn, and receptive. They also had a strong faith in their own abilities. They wanted not only to *know* everything; they wanted to know it better. And they wanted not only to *do* everything, but they wanted to do it as if it had never been done before. They were receptive to the future and intolerant of the past. And lack of tradition means incompetence, not just freedom from prejudice. The role of a teacher was clearly prescribed: to provide access to tradition without curbing enthusiasm for new creation. Unfortunately, one did not fulfil that role as one should have. One also fell victim of the illusion of youth. One believed (although with some reservations) that one was witnessing the process of Western culture's rebirth in Brazil (around new and richer coordinates) and felt enthusiastic about the prospect. New music, poetry, painting, theatre, and ideas sprang up around us like mushrooms after a rain. Deep down, one knew that most of this was useless and unsustainable — hence, in both the classroom and the press one brutally criticised everything. However, one nurtured a hope that this condition was a malady associated with growth and believed in a mature future. A new world was on the horizon.

§ The youth interpreted one's critical attitude as reactionary, and one suffered because of this.

Simultaneously, however one engaged with the youth, so they flocked to us wearing the generous smiles they reserved for those who have been surmounted, but may still have something to offer. Thus, one began to have an influence upon the young and therefore on culture as a whole. One made use of this influence in two ways. One fought against leftist radicalisation, which was cheap and irresponsible. This earned us the label "rightist" from leftist intellectuals, a label one has never managed to shake off. And one tried to awaken a historical consciousness in the youth. This was a problem.

§ One is aware of history's absurdity and one sympathises with trends that seek to overcome historicity and diachrony. However, post-history does not mean pre-history; one could therefore not abide by the pre-historical attitude of the young. He or she who has not heard of the Peloponnesian war cannot intelligently engage in contemporary society. One's attempt to historicise, *malgré soi*, was seen as sterile speculation, "invalid" and "decontextualised." All the same, it fascinated the young because it gave them something they could not get elsewhere: contact with a tradition they unconsciously carried inside themselves. Despite all the doubts and the misunderstandings, those were the best years of one's life: one was playing out the role that was one's calling, that of teacher and leader of youth.

§ Nineteen-sixty-four hit young people like a lightening rod. They did not have a clear view of the situation (that of a country being manipulated from abroad), and so they did not anticipate an event of this magnitude. They rebelled against the efficient military and technocratic apparatus that was gradually established. Although the apparatus was aimed towards several objectives that dovetailed with the youth's own objectives, it nevertheless crushed their fundamental ideals. Their rebellion took on a range of forms, from cultural protests to armed resistance. However, there were two common elements in all of these: they involved personal danger and were extremely inefficient. At the same time, the youth fell victim to irresponsible agitators who used the situation to pursue aims the youth were unaware of. Hence, the academic youth were engaged in a Ping-Pong game between agitation and repression, which gradually undid them. Every day some of them disappeared, and so fear and despair took hold. As a result, the embryo of that new culture (which one now knows would never have seen the light) was terminated. Reality made its triumphal advance against the dream.

§ One saw, therefore, a clear task: to avoid pointless sacrifices and persuade the youth not to throw themselves into senseless adventures. However, one must admit that one's diagnosis of the situation was also mistaken. For several years, one believed this was a temporary phase and that the creative process of culture would resume later in more robust form.

That is why one accepted a mission from the Ministry of Foreign Affairs to go to Europe and the United States in 1966 and 1967 – and hence, my attempt to convince the youth to save their energy for "later." Once one became convinced that "later" no longer made sense, for any of us, one's reasonable advice became meaningless. Those were dark times because one felt the obligation of being a teacher in a situation where one saw no way out. One knew it was necessary to guide the youth, but one did not know how.

§ Simultaneously, the youth transformed quickly and radically. They fell into two groups that could not even be described as opposites. The first was seduced by the apparatus and wanted to become a part of it. They sought a career and bourgeois alienation. One no longer had anything to do with them and there was nothing one could offer. One must also confess, they were of no interest to us either. The second group, overtaken with despair, fell into a "hole" of passivity. This group clinged to us, as if one could point them in the right direction in a situation that offered no way out. One had only two alternatives: to pretend to know the way out or to admit one's powerlessness. Both alternatives were impossible, however, and one's task as a teacher came to an end. One abandoned the youth with a heavy heart. From their point of view, one had betrayed them.

§ Having descended to Dantean depths, this
retrospective must now resurface and ascend
to more bearable heights. The terrace not only
contained the adult nucleus with the young ones
orbiting like planets, it also hosted some occasional
comets – "foreign talents." Whenever there was
a congress, biennial, or an international event of
that sort in São Paulo, some of the participants
made an appearance on the terrace. There is a great
temptation to list some of these sacred cows, since
the reader will know their names. However, one
shall resist, since the role of cows on the terrace
was to be profaned. We learned from them that our
culture left nothing to be desired in comparison to
theirs; we lacked the glory that centres of decision-
making had conferred on them. Some of them
did teach us something, but the primary lesson
was that the terrace was a place that could hold its
own in any context. Cultural "underdevelopment"
is a myth when looked at from the perspective
of the elite. And as for the masses, difference is
a fact, but not in the sense that the masses from
developed countries is "superior" to the ones from
underdeveloped countries. They are merely different.
This retrospective debunks any kind of inferiority
complex: the terrace was the apex of
contemporary culture.

§ And now, it is time to take leave of the terrace.
The dialogues remain inside each participant
and continue to act there. The way in which they
manifest is the key issue. Who knows: perhaps for

some of the participants the dialogues pointed towards some form of engagement, despite everything? In one's own case, the dialogues pointed in a direction that will be discussed in the following chapters.

DISCOURSE

§ At this point in the text I must turn a page and inhale. From now on I shall evoke the complementary aspect of my life: the one in which I sought to change the world. This places me in a difficult situation before the reader. Although I have not yet described my own efforts to change the world, you are already more familiar with them than any other aspect of me for the following reason: my manner of engaging with the world is through "discourse," and the book that you are reading is one of these "discourses." This book is effectively and temporarily the last link in a chain of engagement. This fact is the only aspect of me that you know. You know me as a person who discourses to change the receiver of messages, and you sense my desire to do so as you read. Therefore, even though I have not yet written about my own engagement, you are perfectly aware of it. So I shall reformulate this as a new starting point.

§ Until now, I have tried to describe the world around me and how I oriented myself in it in order to advance against it. From here on I shall describe my own investment and how the world resisted it. This description shall itself be a speculation against the world. Until now, I have written engagedly about my world; now I shall engagedly write about my own engagement with the world. In sum: I have spoken and written about things and people, but now I shall speak and write about my manner of speaking and writing about things for other people.

§ I speak and write with enthusiasm. Speaking and writing are my vices. However, I must add two caveats to this statement. Firstly, I do not entirely submit to these vices; half of me observes the other half, which speaks and writes, in order to control it. Hence, I could say that I rarely lose sight of what I am aspiring to when speaking and writing. Although I become inebriated with words, I do not articulate them in order "to communicate," but "to inform others." Secondly, I am constantly aware that my need to publish is effectively a vice. After every conference in which I read an essay of mine, I feel that bitter taste in my mouth, which is a symptom of "overwhelmed" inebriation. Not only because I always feel as if I have failed, but also because I feel the futility of the effort. I am not exactly an alcoholic. Despite the bitter taste, I speak in order to intensify it so that I never have to speak another word. I want to exhaust the plague of having-to-write, to free myself from it. I do not know if this is a common experience. I only know from my own experience that veritable armies of words constantly rise within me, and they must be ordered and propelled towards others. My only salvation would be the interruption of this "inspired" flow.

§ Obviously, and as I have already mentioned, a psychological diagnosis of my speaking and writing method are of no use to me. I neither want nor need to cure this malady; I must accept it. Since I have been afflicted with the word-plague, it is necessary to transform this vice into an instrument for changing the world and myself. The fact that I sometimes get paid to speak and write is therefore surprising. I believe that I should be punished for speaking and writing – or at least I should have to pay for the permission to speak and write in public. Perhaps, as Guimarães Rosa believed, I *am* paying for it. However, "paying," means something different to me.

§ I cannot clearly distinguish, as two forms of engagement, between speaking and writing and being a teacher and a writer. I speak as if I were writing. An academic class in a Brazilian university has fifty minutes. This was the space I had in which to articulate something. Given this formal challenge, I was inclined to forget that there were students before me. I saw only fifty minutes, just as, with the *Literary Supplement* of the *O Estado de São Paulo* newspaper, I could only see four typewritten pages in my mind. Deleting students from my mind was due in part to the dehumanizing class sizes (more than one hundred students). Curiously, however, the more I forgot about them, the more I gripped their attention.

§ In hindsight, I must have emanated a kind of spell. This is a highly suspect thing, in a Weberian sense: my charisma made me a seducer, not a leader of youth. But I was not aware of this at the time.

I was captivated by the aesthetic challenge of the lecture format, and abandoned everything else to the horizon of my engagement with the world.

§ Obviously, some subjects were imposed upon me. For example, "communication theory" at the Faculty of Communication and Humanities at the A.A. Penteado Foundation and "philosophy of science" at the Polytechnic School of the University of São Paulo. However, these subjects were merely pretexts for the articulation of the equally obligatory spaces. For example, at the Poly: two semesters consisting of a required number of fifty minutes lectures. "Philosophy of science" was the subject to be framed, in order to complete one whole of two semesters, made up of small groups of lectures forming wholes within the greater whole, and with every lecture being an individual, self-sustaining whole. If we missed one lecture, due to a holiday, I despaired. This ruined my overall project. And that is not all. The courses went on for several years, so it was necessary to create an infinite, ascending spiral. "Philosophy of science" was an exciting subject because there was no horizon in sight.

§ My aesthetic attitude, in relation to the courses, was pedagogically suspect; the courses did not correspond with the objectives sought by the establishments that paid me. I shall deal with this issue later, when I discuss my efforts to manipulate the "channels" through which I communicated.

However, I have to confess *a priori* my inability to fit into those establishments. Even when I held the "chair" at the Penteado Foundation, I was still a foreign agent. I was never able to surmount my aversion to any form of academicism. Despite this, I was tolerated for a number of years, because the students demanded my presence (for reasons that did not necessarily coincide with those held by the establishment). However, the students' influence diminished and my position as a "functionary" weakened as a consequence.

§ Although lectures represented my real challenge, I never lost sight of those on the receiving end. I never forgot my aim: to provoke a kind of restlessness in the receivers. In my view, the intellectual's task, generally, and the teacher's task, in particular, is to create zones of intellectual subversion. One day, I found a piece of paper on my desk that said: "My mind is made up; please do not confuse me with facts." This was a triumph for me. The subject of discourse was secondary, in both a formal and existential sense. The important thing was to provoke doubt, which was aesthetically possible. I sought to liberate the youth to become themselves. This meant, in the long run, that my charisma had anti-charismatic effects (my only excuse for it). I will resist the temptation to describe my courses, even though the urge is powerful. I shall sketch only two and sum up the other courses and conferences in a single paragraph at the end of this chapter.

§ Together with Miguel Reale, I planned the structure for a *Studium Generale* (or general studies) school. I had thought about this issue for years and discussed its viability with N. Chomsky, W. Quine, and G. Santillana in Boston. Miguel and I imagined two series of chairs, one for the sciences and the other for the humanities, with a chair for communication theory at the intersection. I will lay out the structure of the project another time, but the chair for communication theory (which I had reserved for myself) not only gave the project a specific purpose, but generated a specific description: "the theory of communication should become the metadiscourse of all forms of human communication, so that the structure of this communication becomes evident." This became the "working definition" for the project at the A.A. Penteado Foundation and resulted in the school's structure and the programme for my course. I will describe the programme here.

§ First, it was necessary to define the scope of the theory's field. Second, it was necessary to classify the phenomena within the field. The classification should be done from several angles in order to give the field depth. Finally, it was necessary to apply the results of the research upon the practice of human communication. The programme is "open" due to the following: (1) the theory's scope is not pre-established; (2) the theory's methods are not pre-established; (3) the praxis for the manipulation of phenomena is not pre-established. The programme's premises are the following: (a) the scope of the theory must be a field that is already part of the scope of other established disciplines; (b) the methods must be borrowed from these disciplines; and (c) the praxis for the manipulation must be original. In sum: "the theory of communication should become the metadiscourse of all forms of human communication, so that the structure of this communication becomes evident in order to be able to change it." A "communicologist" is one who has the instruments at hand for the modification of human communication, and theory is what should provide these instruments. This was the programme for my intended chair.

§ The programme consists of three stages of study. The first stage aims to define its own scope and it is therefore "ontological." It asks: "What is human communication?" The second stage aims to establish research methods and is "epistemological." It asks: "How can human communication be researched?" The third stage aims to find methods to modify the situation of human communication and is "noetically engaged." It asks: "How should human communication work, and what can I do with it?" The programme makes two aspects evident: (a) thus defined, the theory of communication is not "exempt from value" (scientific), but is "engaged with value" (humanistic); (b) thus defined, the theory of communication is a *Studium*

Generale because it synthesises several disciplines, generalising them in order to de-automate and de-technologise them while conserving their "exact" character. Thus defined, the theory of communication aims to overcome technocratic learning in exchange for a type of learning that is humanistically engaged.

§ I varied the different stages of the programme during several courses. I proposed new criteria for the definition of the field and therefore new methods for the classification of the field. And my students and I always attempted to influence the communication channels that surrounded us. I will give several examples.

§ For one of the courses, I made use of the phenomenological approach as a criterion to distinguish between human communication and other types of phenomena. This led us to distinguish between "culture" and "nature," using human gesture as a criterion, as the articulation of human interiority, and as an expression of "freedom." It was necessary to define "gesture" as a class of "motions by the human body." The human body became a problem. Afterwards, it was necessary to distinguish between at least two types of "gesture": acted on a thing and gesture towards another person. The first type was called "work" and the second "intersubjective communication." The communication channel for the first type was called "artwork" and the second "gesture itself."

The scope of the theory thus became the totality of gestures as articulations of freedom.

§ For another course, I made use of existential analysis as a criterion to distinguish between human communication and other types of phenomena. We made a distinction between "being together" (the other) and "being at hand" (the thing). Thus, human communication was defined as ways of "being together." Among the ways of being together, one emerged as fundamental: the convention that "makes sense of things," therefore, the interhuman codification process that conventionalises certain things into "symbols." Every other type of human communication is founded upon this one. Then the problem of codification without a previously existent code emerged, which means "the origin of communication." The scope of the theory became defined as the totality of codes (therefore, the dimension of the human "spirit").

§ I cannot continue, for lack of space, to enumerate all the propositions for the definition of the theory's scope. I shall only mention that the Marxist criteria (the dialectic man versus thing) proved fruitful, but could not be elaborated upon for fear of "snitches" among the students in the class.

§ As for classification of the field's scope, I shall mention some of the categories: (a) Nerves (audio, visual, tactile, olfactory communication, etc.). Methods: physiology, behaviourism, etc. (b) Function (mass, elite, closed circuit communication, etc.). Methods: sociology, social psychology, etc. (c) Dynamic (discourse, dialogue, irradiation, tree, ellipsis communication, etc.). Methods: cybernetics, game theory, etc. (d) Symbol (denotative, connotative, imaginative, conceptual communication, etc.). Methods: literary criticism, aesthetics, etc. (e) Information (original, banal, kitsch communication, etc.). Methods: information theory, etc. (f) Message (imperative, indicative, exclamatory, inquisitive communication, etc.). Methods: logical analysis, etc. (g) Channels (unidimensional, multidimensional, diachronic, synchronic communication, etc.). Methods: *Gestalt* psychology, etc. (h) Social (work, consumer, entertainment communication, etc.). Methods: economy, sociology, etc. ... and so on and so forth.

§ What matters in relation to this classification is how the methods overlapped, and I will give an example. We compared a television programme on zoology with a middle school zoology book. We classified both in several ways. The result was surprising. We discovered, especially in the book's case, several "ideological" layers in both the message and in other, unsuspected forms. We had the feeling of having entered unknown territory and we became explorers, despite the pre-existing literature on the subject. Our work was mostly lost, however, not only because anything outside general trends in the current Brazilian situation tends to be ignored, but because academic work tends to disappear in the avalanche of generalised super-production. Photocopies of lectures are kept in dusty corners of the foundation's library, as well as in so many libraries around the world. Dwelling on the volume of energy and creative fantasy lying dormant around the world drives one into despair, in thinking about engaging with culture.

§ In terms of manipulating communication around us, I will discuss some of the study groups we formed: (a) restructuring the subject chair; (b) restructuring the lectures' dynamics; (c) restructuring the school (d) restructuring the press through my essays and my students' essays; (e) restructuring magazines through my essays and through magazines edited by my students; (f) restructuring television by me and a group of students; (g) actions upon theatre, films, and advertising by some of my students; (h) producing exhibitions, round-table discussions, happenings, etc. by my assistants; (i) my attempt to restructure the São Paulo Art Bienal. Summing up the results, we found two types of resistance. One was the environment's inertia. The other was the highly efficient manipulation of the existing system, which was the decisive one. We sought to manipulate communication in order to free the message receiver from the channels' tyranny, and the system sought to manipulate communication in order to further subjugate the message receiver in more exact ways. Given such an unequal struggle, we were defeated. I will speak about (f) the television and (i) the Bienal later in the book since these two examples are quite revealing.

§ Following are the results of my engagement with the chair of "communication theory": (a) <u>Positive</u>: I learned a lot. I formed a productive friendship with my two assistants, Gabriel Borba and Alan Meyer. I met some exceptional people among my students and exerted some influence on them. I also had the opportunity to systematically develop some ideas. (b) <u>Negative</u>: I did not become part of the establishment. I felt aversion towards the game of personal status that my colleagues played. The majority of my students sought merely a diploma and a career, which depressed me. I had an unwittingly charismatic effect on the students. The school's intellectual level was exasperating. And my efforts to change the situation were thwarted.
§ In hindsight, the thought of returning to that chair position is a nightmare. I did not want to go through that experience, but it meant experiencing the Brazilian situation, and international academia.

Philosophy of Science

§ Milton Vargas, who wanted to achieve a similar kind of *Studium Generale*, ran the course on the philosophy of science at the Polytechnic School of the University of São Paulo. Our intention was to erect a series of subjects that would act as barriers, vertically cutting through the school's horizontal course-structure and thus forcing every student, in every specialisation – from electronics to naval construction – to study these subjects. The belief was that this method would impose upon the future technologist and functionary a "general and humanistic view of the world." Articulated this way, our intention sounds absurd: to technically manipulate technologists in order to "humanise them." I believe that this absurdity characterises every technocratic effort in favour of "humanity." At the school, it became palpable.

§ Acting as a substitute for Vargas at the school, I occupied a subaltern position. My task was to deliver lectures and not worry about the curriculum structure. In this regard, my responsibility and ability to act were less than at the A.A. Penteado Foundation. However, something happened (never officially recognised), which caused the curriculum to slice vertically across the school, as well as wider parts of the University. Hundreds of students attended my class, sitting on the ground and around my chair and forming what was, for me, an amorphous mass. When I determined to find out where these students were coming from, I discovered that, although my course was required for the students at the Polytechnic, many did not attend and falsified "attendance sheets." However, there were many students (and professors) in attendance in my class, from Philosophy, Biology, and Law. And there was something sinister

around this: for years, this was denied, even as
it was happening. Thinking of it now makes me
shudder. This was so sinister to me that I did not
even discuss it with Vargas. A kind of prudishness
prevented me from doing so.

§ The heterogeneous nature of the students had an
effect on the course. Initially, I intended to teach
a course aimed at technicians and the subject was
to be the problematic region between science and
technics, in which knowledge becomes praxis and
pure "research" becomes engagement in favour
of Man and society. Given the group's make up,
however, I changed the subject. I turned the course
into a tribunal from which I could exert influence
on a representative group of São Paulo's academic
youth. I broadened the subject, but without
losing sight of the original aim. I sought to frame
science as a discourse that accumulates "objective"
explanations of phenomena, and as a historically
defined method to humanise nature and naturalise
humanity. I sought, therefore, to demonstrate to
the young the current rupture between formalism
and historicism (and structuralism and Marxism)
using science as a central theme. Simultaneously,
I sought to position the philosophy of science
within the wider context of a generalised theory
of communication. In doing so, I took on a
structuralist point of view, but I sought, as much
as the circumstances allowed, to do justice to the
Marxist arguments against this point of view. I
must clarify this point a little, however, both from

the perspective of my own biography and the circumstances of the course.

§ I have already mentioned my dual approach to communication theory: from my obsession with language and from a philosophy of science, as I understood it. Strictly speaking, there was no duplicity here. In my view, science has always been a method of speaking and the philosophy of science is therefore a component of the philosophy of language. Although, I have to say, science was the component that tended to consume the other parts like a cancer. I believe the philosophy of science will only find its place within a not-yet-developed theory of communication.

§ Ever since reading Schlick in Prague, I was convinced that science is essentially a discourse. However, science always assumed an entirely different role in relation to language than the Neopositivists' argued. For them, language is a map that mirrors circumstances (*Sachverhalte*), and that is why, for the Neopositivists, there are only two problems: (a) what can, or cannot, be mirrored by language? And (b) how can I distinguish between correct, incorrect, and blind mirroring (between true, false, and nonsensical propositions)? The result of this approach is that, for the Neopositivists, science becomes the only valid method of speaking – or, at least, a very privileged one. For me, language is something else. When I spoke of Wittgenstein, I stated that, for me, language is like a plague that acts diabolically inside us, alienating us from reality. Simultaneously (as a consequence), language is our dignity. Language has a clear, religious colouring. I will return to this when I discuss *Language and Reality* and *The History of the Devil*. I therefore approached the Marxist interpretation of science as a tool for destroying reality from the inside out, and reformulated it according to linguistic rules (the rules of thought). In my view, scientific propositions do not reflect real situations. On the contrary, reality is broken down into situations through the corruptive (analysing) action of scientific discourse. Ultimately, I think Wittgenstein (and some Marxists) would agree. But both, I fear, may lose sight of the decisive element of this process: the poetic power of language. For me, science is *poiesis*, in a diabolic sense: the formal breakdown of reality. This does not necessarily condemn me to Manichaeism, however, as the following argument will show.

§ I read books grounded in logical positivism, Marxism, and existential analysis; Kant in the original and via Cassirer's writings; and Jaspers, begrudgingly. In the background, Nietzsche and Dewey were lying in wait. And in the foreground was the trend towards autonomy in the sciences and technocratic fascism, as prophesied by Marcuse and Arendt. It was, to repeat, in this diabolical climate that my dialogues with Vicente, Vargas, and Leônidas Hegenberg, which I will now outline, took place.

§ Like me, Vicente was focused on the philosophy of science from the viewpoint of logical positivism and existential analysis, and he reached a place not entirely different from my own – although within a different sphere. For him, science was an aspect of the Western project and it obscured reality. Therefore, it alienated Western Man from reality, transforming Man into a subject and reality into a collection of objects. It profaned reality. The germ of science lies in Judeo-Christianity. Scientific discourse is nothing but a progressive development from this germ. However, the real project, which established science, is transhuman: it is the disclosure of a negative establishing power. In the West, Nothingness reveals itself as a Divinity and science progressively realises this nullifying power.

§ Vicente's terrifying view differed from my own because his was "reactionary" in its structure. For him, scientific progress distances us from the Sacred. For me, scientific progress is how Man affirms, although diabolically, his dignity in the face of reality. In my view, however, Vicente's vision had the virtue of clearly framing the problem of science within the appropriate coordinates: religion. I had to digest Vicente (and Heidegger and Nietzsche along with him).

§ Vargas' attitude in relation to science was entirely different from Vicente's. I shall not elaborate upon his philosophy of science here, since he is still working on it. However, he has three arguments that must be cited, since they influence me: (a) the specific character of scientific propositions; (b) the trans-historicity of the propositions; and (c) the historically-defined character of modern science. The apparent contradiction between (b) and (c) will be eliminated in the following argument. (a) The weight of "truth" in scientific propositions is different from that of philosophical propositions. Scientific propositions are "restricted" in the sense of being truthful in relation to particular situations. And they are "universal" in the sense they are truthful to anyone who accepts science as a method for obtaining knowledge. Philosophical propositions pretend to be universally valid, but can be contested by philosophy itself. Scientific propositions do not pretend to be universal, but are scientifically incontestable. (b) Scientific propositions are formally true. That is why they can be "falsified" if they are "true." This statement should be expanded upon. It stands in opposition to current formalism, which maintains that in order to be scientific, propositions must be "falsifiable." For example, for T. Kuhn, after every "structural revolution," propositions that were previously "true" become nonsense. It also stands in opposition to any type of historicism – for example, the dialectic type, according to which Einstein replaced Newton. Vargas does not consider "science" the part of Newton that was replaced by Einstein, and so, in his view, Einstein has not replaced the scientific Newton. For him, science is therefore a cumulative process of "eternal" truths.

To me, this argument is robust and disturbing. (c) Despite this, science is a historically defined human activity. Modern science emerged during the Baroque period and has a Baroque character. An analysis of its structure reveals this underlying character. The Renaissance possessed the germ of another kind of science, which was never realised. Leonardo da Vinci, not Galileo, could have been the founder of modern science – and with it, fantasy and not intellectual experimentation could have been the foundational method. Due to this, science lost one dimension but it did not cease being "formally true." However, modern science only grasps that portion of reality the Baroque attitude allows. These arguments had to be included in my course.

§ Leônidas Hegenberg is a philosophy professor at the Institute of Technology for Aeronautics (which is a kind of Brazilian MIT). We became friends when I delivered a series of lectures at the Institute in São José dos Campos. He is a logical positivist from the period after the crisis brought on by Popper. I will not discuss his opinions or our disagreements about "theories" at the Brazilian Institute of Philosophy, which were published separately in the institute's magazine. What matters is that we discussed the course at the Polytechnic and I took into consideration his suggestions and arguments.

§ I will outline the course here. I started with the premise that modern science is a specific discourse, both in relation to its symbols and its structure. The symbols have a denotative function (they are clear and distinct) and the structure is the same as logics and mathematics, which are constantly under development. The foundation of the discourse is more or less an unconscious convention – the consequence of being a particular form of "being together" (*Mitsein*), which is characteristic of the Western bourgeoisie. In this sense, science is a type of bourgeois communication. Therefore, it may be analysed on two levels: at the level of discourse, through the methods of logical positivism, and at the level of conventional codification, through the methods of materialist dialectic. Science is thus accessible to both formalism and historicism. However, neither of these methods can damage its core: the mysterious fact that science "knows" and "works."

§ In my course, I linked the epistemological mystery to the greater one of the human capacity to create symbols, but I did not attempt to "explain it." I attempted to show how science, as well as art, philosophy, and religion cast a net of symbols around Man, a net that subsequently becomes "true" because it mysteriously replaces reality. The dialectic of this replacement (the fact that symbols that veil and unveil meanings) is its truth. Only science emits propositions that replace reality in a different manner from other propositions, because it is based on a different convention. They are intersubjectively true to anyone who accepts its conventionalised codification and they are nonsense to anyone who does not accept it. Accepting this codification is not the consequence of a deliberate act. We are obliged to accept it because it represents the expression of our *being-in-the-world* – in other words, being 20th-century bourgeois. We must accept the conventions of science because we are what we are. That is why scientific propositions are necessarily true for us.

§ The philosophy of science is the effort to overcome ourselves and see ourselves from the outside. We cannot afford to *not* "believe" in science (this is a question of creed, and science is a religious phenomenon). However, we can see our creed from the outside and compare it with others. Then we will grasp science as a communicative net we live in, and upon which we act. The philosophy of science could have, therefore, at least two uses: first, it could demythologise science (de-scientify it) by showing us that it is not "the" truth but "our" truth. Second, it could withdraw the autonomy of science (making it technocratic no longer) by showing that it is a human form of *being-in-the-world*. However, philosophy is not able to diminish our fear in the face of the fundamental mystery that Man is a being in whom ordering symbols and structures are generated; fright in the face of diabolical human alienation. Philosophy can show that science is a historically-defined human activity, but it is obliged to leave the origins of this activity in mysterious darkness.

§ The miracle of technics, the constantly renewable and insurmountable surprise that symbolic equations are translatable to reality and function there, I saw as equally inexplicable. I only sought to shed some light on this miracle. In doing so, I was attempting to dispute the tendency to see technology as magic. I considered Wittgenstein's statement, according to which everything obeys the laws of science – otherwise they would not be "things." I tried to demonstrate how the laws of science do not "unveil" the structures of nature, but impose these structures upon it; that "to know" does not mean "to discover" something, but "to impose order." However, I capitulated that some systems function better than others: to go to the Moon, it is more intelligent to position ourselves according to Einstein's equations than to Anthroposophy. That is the miracle.

§ Even in this case, however, philosophy can be detached and shed light upon the miracle, externally. First, it can show that the miracle of technics is nothing but a special case in the greater miracle of "praxis" – or the human capacity to dip its toe into reality. Philosophy can demonstrate that "technics" is nothing but the historically conditioned manifestation, simultaneously, of human transcendence and immanence, and that it is not necessarily a new phenomenon. Technics is not the miracle; the human situation is. On the other hand, philosophy can show that technics, as the manipulation of reality, is disinterested, since it does not manipulate "reality," but manipulates phenomena conceived *ad hoc*. The purpose of technics is to change humanity, which possesses it, and not manipulate things or turn humans into things. The purpose of technics is to change humans through their own praxis. Therefore, philosophy can humanise technics and avoid the technologising of humans. I believe this is the core of any real kind of Marxism. However, the majority of Marxists tend to discount the mystery behind the mere possibility of praxis.

§ This was, approximately, the message of my course. I no longer agree with it in every detail. Today, I would change several features. But I still support its foundation: on the one hand, to fight the tendency to make everything scientific and technocratic (fascist tendencies), by demystifying science and its alienating function; on the other, to preserve fear in the face of the mystery that makes science and every type of human communication possible. The course was therefore a component of my engagement with the groundlessness in which I found myself: a struggle against surrounding circumstances and a search for grounding.

§ Externally, the course stagnated, due to academic formalities couched in personal resentments fomented by the Brazilian situation. The course was transferred to the Philosophy Faculty of the University of São Paulo, hacked up, and put in the hands of my curiously leftist "enemies." Internally, however, the course stagnated, not because it did not fit into the smaller context (the University), or the larger one (the Brazilian situation). It died a natural death because I was excluded, by osmosis, and because I extracted myself from the school. I do not believe, however, that I was entirely ineffectual. Some of the students who attended the course will become functionaries and technocrats in the future, but with a slightly disturbed conscience.

CPSIA information can be obtained
at www.ICGtesting.com
Printed in the USA
LVHW050825170921
698050LV00022B/1474

9 780993 327261